DEVOTIONS TO TAKE YOU Deeper

OTHER BOOKS IN THE GROWING 2:52 LIBRARY

2:52 Boys Bible

NIV 2:52 Backpack Bible

Devotions to Make You Stronger

Devotions to Make You Smarter

Bible Freaks & Geeks

Seriously Sick Bible Stuff

Creepy Creatures & Bizarre Beasts from the Bible

Bible Heroes & Bad Guys

Bible Angels & Demons

Big Bad Bible Giants

Bible Wars & Weapons

Weird & Gross Bible Stuff

How to Draw Big Bad Bible Beasts

How to Draw Good, Bad & Ugly Bible Guys

DEVOTIONS TO TAKE YOU Deeper

ED STRAUSS

ZONDERVAN.com/
AUTHORTRACKER
follow your favorite authors

 ZONDERkidz™

Requests for information should be addressed to:
Zonderkidz, *Grand Rapids, Michigan 49530*

Library of Congress Cataloging-in-Publication Data

Strauss, Ed, 1953-
Devotions to take you deeper : by Ed Strauss.
p. cm -- (2:52)
ISBN-13: 978-0-310-71313-5 (softcover)
ISBN-10: 0-310-71313-7 (softcover)
1. Boys -- Prayers and devotions I. Title.
BV4855.S775 2007
242'.62--dc22

2007030934

Editor: Barbara Scott
Art direction and design: Merit Alderink

Printed in the United States of America

07 08 09 10 11 12 • 10 9 8 7 6 5 4 3 2 1

table of contents

devotion #1

SEEING THAT GOD IS REAL

God's invisible qualities — his eternal power and divine nature — have been clearly seen, being understood from what has been made.

— Romans 1:20

God is a spiritual being. He lives in another dimension, and human eyeballs just aren't made for seeing spiritual things. That whole realm is invisible to us. Even if you had night-vision goggles, you still couldn't see God. But there *is* a way to clearly understand what he's like. How's that? By looking at the world that God made.

When you play a super cool computer game with cutting-edge graphics, you just *know* that some awesome programmer designed the thing, right?

Even if the programmer's not around for you to actually see, you know he or she exists. If you walk into your friend's house and see a million-piece Lego castle, you might ask, "Whoa! Did you build this?" If your friend says, "Nah. The dog sneezed, and this all fell into place," you'd say, "Yeah, riiight."

It's the same with God. Study the awesome way that nature works and how complex living things are, and it hits you that you're looking at the work of an invisible, intelligent Creator. And this Creator's not just super smart, he has awesome power. When people examine things like DNA or the human brain, even if they don't know God, they figure there *had* to be an intelligent designer behind it. It's far too amazing to be an accident.

Do you want to see evidence of God? Look at the things he created. They tell you a lot about what he's like and give you a glimpse of how powerful he is.

devotion #2

ONE GOD - ONE WAY TO HEAVEN

"Salvation is found in no one else, for there is no other name under heaven given to men by which we must be saved."

— Acts 4:12

If you want to please God and live forever in heaven, first you have to figure out who God is. So, who is the true god? Were the ancient *Greeks* right when they said that when you leave this life you will live in Elysium with Zeus? Nope. Well then, how about the ancient Scandinavians who said that you will live in Valhalla with Thor? No. This verse tells us that there's only *one* God who brings salvation — the God of the Bible. All other so-called gods are imposters.

Now, how do you find salvation with the one true God? What do you have to do to make sure that you end up in heaven? If you brush your teeth faithfully four hundred times a day, rake leaves off every driveway in your city, and rescue at least forty cats from trees, will *that* do it? No. Those things will wear you out, but they won't get you into heaven. So what's the way?

Jesus said, "I am the way." He added, "No one comes to the Father except through me" (John 14:6). Okay, *now* we're zeroing in on how to find salvation. You have to go through Jesus! In fact, the Bible makes it very clear: "If you confess with your mouth, 'Jesus is Lord,' and believe in your heart that God raised him from the dead, you will be saved" (Romans 10:9).

Praying to Zeus won't save you. Being the best Boy Scout on the block won't save you. Only believing in Jesus gives you eternal life.

devotion #3

HOW WE GOT THE BIBLE

"How did you come to write all this? Did Jeremiah dictate it?"

"Yes," Baruch replied, "he dictated all these words to me, and I wrote them in ink on the scroll."

— Jeremiah 36:17–18

How did we get the Bible? The words in the Bible were inspired by God. In some cases, God spoke directly to prophets like Moses who wrote down his words. And Jeremiah spent forty years repeating God's exact words to his scribe Baruch and the people of Judah. Jeremiah was even put into jail for the difficult news he spoke, but he continued to repeat God's message. And later in ancient Israel, flocks of scribes had the job of making exact copies of the prophets' books. So, we have a reliable record of God's Word.

Has a teacher ever given you a complicated explanation that you didn't write down? Then when you tried to remember it later, you forgot it completely, remembered only a word or two, or got it totally mixed up. And memory loss even hits with short, simple messages! Think how many times you say to your mom, "Yeah, I'll do it," but a minute later *whatever* she said is totally wiped out of your mind.

That's why God had his prophets write down what he said right away. God inspired many prophets and writers because he wanted to be sure that people knew what he was telling them. So, people like you, living today, know *exactly* what he wants you to do.

Thank God for ink and scrolls and paper! Thank God for prophets and scribes who knew how to write! Thank God that these words have been preserved and delivered to us. That's how we got the Bible.

devotion #4

THE HOLY SPIRIT'S POWER

"You will receive power when the Holy Spirit comes on you."

— Acts 1:8

What's this? Receiving power? *That* sounds good — like a superpower! But who is this Holy Spirit? The Holy Spirit is also called the Spirit of God, and Jesus promised his disciples that after he went to heaven he'd send the Spirit of God himself into their hearts — to live inside them! Wow! No wonder you get power! When God's Spirit enters you, you admit the most powerful being in the universe into your life.

There are lots of movies and cartoons about kids receiving superpowers. Someone gets bombarded with radiation, or a genetically altered spider bites him, and the next thing you know he

can walk up walls, bend steel bars, or surround himself with a force field. Of course, on top of going to school and doing homework, these superheroes have to wear colorful costumes and go out and save the world!

Although superheroes aren't real, what the Bible says about God filling you with the power of his Holy Spirit is real. Of course, God probably won't give you the ability to climb up skyscrapers. God gives his Spirit so that you'll have power to live like a Christian. His Spirit also comforts you when you're afraid or sad. The Holy Spirit teaches you how to pray and guides you in your choices. The Spirit also helps you tell others about Jesus.

God's Spirit can give you power, and you *need* that power. So, pray and ask God to help you access the power of the Holy Spirit, so you can begin to live a stronger Christian life.

Devotion #5

TALKING TO GOD ALL DAY LONG

Pray continually; give thanks in all circumstances, for this is God's will for you.

—1 Thessalonians 5:17–18

Pray continually? Does that mean I'm supposed to stumble around on my knees with my eyes shut? Nice try, buddy. You won't even make it across the street if you try *that* stunt. Praying continually means that you can talk to God no matter what you're doing. And prayer isn't just asking God for stuff. Often it's a quick thank you to God. Sometimes it simply means being *aware* of God and wanting to obey him.

When you hear the words "prayer time," what comes to your mind? Saying twenty seconds worth of grace over left-over pasta? Yawning bedside prayers for forty seconds? Those things are prayer,

true, but with 1,440 minutes in a day, don't you have more time for God than one minute? God is your best friend, and he's with you all day long. If you spent all day with one of your friends, you'd talk to him a *lot*, right?

So communicate with God. He wants to hear from you. Prayer is talking honestly and respectfully to God, and you should do that whatever else you're doing — whether you're lying down to sleep, making a tough decision, or white-water rafting with your eyes wide open. Yes, it's okay to pray with your eyes open.

God is always here listening, and he has the power to answer your prayers. So stay in close communication with him.

devotion #6

KEEPING A CLEAR CONSCIENCE

"I strive always to keep my conscience clear before God and man."

— Acts 24:16

God has given everybody on earth a conscience. It's part of the package. A conscience is your mind knowing the difference between right and wrong. When you do wrong, your conscience makes you feel bad. When you do what's right, you have peace. The apostle Paul said he tried to keep a clear conscience by doing what was right before God *and* before people.

If you think that a conscience is a tiny angel fluttering at your right ear telling you to do good, and a tiny devil at your left ear tempting you to lie or take a cookie, you've been watching

way too much TV. A conscience is the knowledge that certain things are right and certain things are wrong. For example, your conscience tells you that caring for the weak is right, honoring your parents is right, but stealing is wrong.

When you're tempted to do wrong, your conscience reminds you that it's wrong. If you go ahead and do it anyway, your conscience kicks in again, making you feel guilty. If you apologize to the person you wronged, then you have a clear conscience again. And guess what? If you have a clear conscience and obey God's commands, you can be confident that God will answer your prayers. (See 1 John 3:21 – 22.) That's one of the benefits of having a clear conscience!

Your conscience is a gift from God. Don't ignore it. When it tells you to do something good, obey it. When your conscience tells you *not* to do something bad, well, *duh*, don't.

Devotion #7

JESUS' POWERFUL RESURRECTION

"He was not abandoned to the grave, nor did his body see decay. God has raised this Jesus to life, and we are all witnesses of the fact."

— Acts 2:31 – 32

Jesus was nailed to a cross on a Friday morning, and he died that afternoon. His friends buried him just before sunset, and Jesus' lifeless body lay in a cold, dark tomb all that night, all the next day, and all the *next* night. Then at dawn Sunday morning, there was a violent earthquake, the stone door of his tomb rolled aside, and Jesus walked out. He appeared to his disciples, proving that he was alive again.

You may say, "Okay, I saw a program about a guy on TV whose heart stopped. He was dead for two minutes, and then the doctors gave him an electric shock, and he came back to life." Yeah, but that guy wasn't nearly beaten to death by Roman soldiers and then nailed to a cross. And he didn't lay dead in a tomb for about forty hours. When people are dead like Jesus was dead, they're good and dead and they *stay* dead.

Another thing: when Jesus' body came back to life, his flesh-and-blood corpse was transformed into a powerful, eternal body that could walk through walls or appear and disappear. His body had been utterly changed. This was a supernatural miracle.

Jesus is the only person who ever actually died, rose from the dead, and now lives forever! His resurrection was a huge, convincing proof that he was who he claimed to be — God's Son.

devotion #8

WHY WE WORSHIP GOD

To him who loves us and has freed us from our sins by his blood ... to him be glory and power for ever and ever!

— Revelation 1:5–6

Why does the Bible tell us to worship God? Does God have an ego problem? Does he need people to constantly repeat how great he is? No. Worship simply means recognizing how awesome God is — and *saying* it. We worship Jesus because he's God's Son, and he loved us enough to die for us *and* was powerful enough to return to life. Does Jesus get proud when we praise him? No. He said, "I am gentle and humble in heart" (Matthew 11:29).

Imagine your dad works in the Air Force, and one day he gives you high-level clearance and takes you into the super secret hangar of the newest experimental jet. (You *wish*!) You walk in and there's this shimmering, monstrous, powerful *thing*! Your eyes bug out, and you shout, "Whoa! Awesome!" Some things are jaw-dropping awesome.

God is far, far more powerful and awesome than that, and his Holy Spirit packs way more power! And what Jesus did by dying to save us and then coming back to life deserves our praise! *Is* Jesus glorious? Yes. *Is* Jesus powerful? You bet he is. So when we worship God, we're simply recognizing how fantastic he is.

When you realize how awesome God is and what fantastic things he has done for you, and you're in awe and feeling grateful—that's worship.

Devotion #9

SAVAGE APPROACH TO BIBLE READING

The lions roar for their prey and seek their food from God. The sun rises, and they steal away; they return and lie down in their dens.

— Psalm 104:21–22

If you're a lion, you spend your time tracking down food. And when you spot a delicious four-legged lunch, you sneak up on it, rush it, leap on it, and take it down. Then you bite off chunks and swallow them. When your belly is full, you flop yourself down in some shady, bone-littered cave, belch, blink your eyes the way lions do, and digest.

You can do that with the Bible too. You get hungry to know

something about God, so you grab your Bible, flop down on your bed, and go hunting through its pages. It's like moving through the grass. Then when you spot an interesting truth, you leap on it and begin devouring it. You spend some time eating it. You don't just lick it once and walk past. Then you blink and think, "Now, how does that apply to my life today?"

That's the savage approach to Bible reading, and it works for some people. You move when hunger strikes; you get up and go after some truth. Of course, some people like to read devotions at the same time every morning or evening. Fine. Do that. But when you get a sudden hunger for truth, there's nothing like prowling in your Bible.

Have you gone hunting for wisdom and truth today? Have you lain back in some cave and digested what the verses mean? Go for it today.

Devotion #10

THE PLANET OF MISSING SOCKS

"Do not store up for yourselves treasures on earth . . . But store up for yourselves treasures in heaven."

— Matthew 6:19–20

Jesus said not to work hard to pile up treasures on earth. Why? Well, for one thing, they won't last. Moths might eat your clothes (except for the buttons), rust can ruin your toys, and thieves can steal your money. I mean, think about it. Your socks even get lost inside the washing machine — *all the time*. Earth's just a bad place to store treasure. It makes a lot more sense to stack up treasures in heaven.

Sure, you do need food, clothes, and a place to live. Nobody is saying

that you don't. You need gym shoes, and you need a toothbrush. (You also need to *use* your toothbrush.) Yes, you even need toys and fun times. Jesus knows you need all these things. He didn't forget that. So what does he mean when he says not to pile up treasure on earth?

It means that although you might wow other kids with how many toys and collectibles you can fill your bedroom with, things get old, they get broken or ripped or — like your socks — go missing. Also, a year from now you may not even be interested in those kinds of things.

You need some treasures on earth. Just don't pile them up. Don't let them crowd God out of your life. You need treasures in heaven even more. Start storing up treasures in heaven with your service to God. After all, you'll live there forever!

Devotion #11

HAVE MERCY – FORGIVE OTHERS

"If you do not forgive men their sins, your Father will not forgive your sins."

— Matthew 6:15

Once a guy owed a king millions of dollars, so the king ordered that he, his family, and everything he owned be sold to pay the debt. The man begged for mercy, so the king forgave the whole debt. Then that guy found a fellow who owed him a few thousand bucks and demanded he pay. The fellow begged for mercy, but the first guy threw him in prison. The king was furious. He asked, "Shouldn't you have had mercy on your fellow servant just as I had on you?" (Matthew 18:21–35).

If you're like most kids, you've broken quite a few of God's commandments — sometimes day after day. But if you accept that Jesus died on the cross for your sins and ask God to forgive you, you're forgiven. God doesn't hold your sins against you. So then what do you do when your brother accidentally breaks your Lego model? Punch him? Tell him he's never allowed in your room again?

The point of Jesus' parable is this: God has been merciful to us and has forgiven us for many sins, so we need to turn around and be merciful to those who sin against us. If we don't forgive others when they offend or hurt us, God won't forgive us *our* sins. He may let us suffer the consequences of our mistakes to teach us a lesson.

God prefers to forgive. He'd rather not discipline you. So be merciful to others, just like God has been merciful to you.

devotion #12

GARLIC PEELS, ZITS, AND MESSY HAIR

Anyone who listens to the word but does not do what it says is like a man who looks at his face in a mirror and . . . goes away and immediately forgets what he looks like.

— James 1:23–24

People in New Testament times had mirrors too, and before they stepped out of their houses, they checked themselves out. If they had a garlic peel on their teeth, they picked it off. If they had a zit, they popped it. If their hair was uncombed, they combed it. But James talked about people who read God's Word and saw what they should do, but mumbled, "Yeah, yeah," and then walked off and forgot about it.

You may not be too concerned about what you look like before you rush out the door. Maybe you just want to dash out the door to play. But it pays to care. Otherwise you'll run out to play baseball with jam on your face, your hair standing straight up, or your T-shirt on backward. So get in the habit of looking in the mirror and then fixing what needs fixing.

Even more importantly, you should care what you look like on the inside. How do you do that? Read the Bible—especially chapters like 1 Corinthians 13—to see how God wants your heart to look. Compare your thinking and your actions to how the Bible says a Christian ought to behave. Then do what it says to do.

When you see that you need to fix some areas of your life, fix them. Don't just say, "Yeah, yeah," and forget about it. Read God's Word and obey it.

devotion #13

PART OF THE PRIDE

Pursue righteousness, faith, love and peace, along with those who call on the Lord out of a pure heart.

— 2 Timothy 2:22

To *pursue* means "to chase or to follow." You know, like a lion pursues a zebra across the savannah. (Run, zebra! Run!) So the Bible tells you to set your sights on good stuff like righteousness, faith, love, and peace — and then to chase those things nonstop. And don't just go after these things alone. Just like lions hunt in teams, it works best when you pursue good stuff with other Christians. (Scratch one zebra.)

There's an old saying: "If you run with wolves, you'll learn to howl like a

wolf." Well, if you run with weasels, you'll start squeaking like a weasel. The point is that if you spend time with a bad crowd, they influence you, right? Hang with a smoking, cursing crowd, and the odds are you'll end up smoking and swearing. (At least you'll be breathing second-hand smoke and getting an earful of curses.) Or if your friends watch sick movies, they'll try to suck you into that too.

It's great to have cool friends who do exciting stuff, but remember: you *can* do cool, fun stuff with Christians. Believers can have lots of fun too! It's okay to have non-Christian friends, but your closest pals should be other Christians — you know, guys "who call on the Lord." The fun stuff you do can include praying with them and studying the Bible together. Instead of getting into all the wrong stuff, these dudes are doing what's right. So run with lions — not with weasels.

devotion #14

JESUS' POWER OVER DEMONS

When he saw Jesus, he cried out and fell at his feet, shouting at the top of his voice, "What do you want with me, Jesus, Son of the Most High God? I beg you, don't torture me!"

— Luke 8:28

A long time ago in Israel, a demon-possessed madman lived in a graveyard beside the Sea of Galilee. Then Jesus' boat landed. When the Son of God stepped ashore, the guy rushed out from the tombs to meet him. One look at Jesus, and the demons inside this guy went bonkers. The guy fell down and began screaming at the top of his voice to Jesus, "I beg you, don't torture me!" Right away Jesus cast the devils out of him.

Some movies and comic books have things totally backward. They describe demons and evil spirits as mighty, fearsome beings — which some of them are — but the way they have it, it's usually only some bigger demon who can finally beat them. Modern comic and movie scriptwriters have totally forgotten what the Bible says.

When Jesus met demons, the demons trembled with terror, flopped to the ground, and wailed and begged him not to punish them. When the Son of God looked them in the eyes, they screamed and shrieked and went crazy with fear.

So who's the most powerful? Jesus! You don't have to be afraid of the devil or demons because this same powerful Jesus is still protecting us today.

devotion #15

ANGELS ON UNDERCOVER ASSIGNMENTS

Do not forget to entertain strangers, for by so doing some people have entertained angels without knowing it.

— Hebrews 13:2

The Bible says that angels are powerful, spiritual beings who bring messages from heaven. Angels are not humans, and people don't turn into angels when they die, but sometimes angels appear on earth in human form so that they won't stand out in the crowd.

We can only imagine what angels look like, and movies provide some of our ideas. What picture comes to mind when you think of an angel? Maybe you see a blond guy in a long white robe with giant wings sprouting from

his shoulder blades. Maybe he even has a glowing Frisbee over his head. Or maybe you think an angel might come down to earth, fall in love, and decide to become human.

Although the Bible tells us that angels wore robes in Bible times, that's what everybody else was wearing back then. Who knows what angels are wearing today? And though we usually picture angels with wings, the Bible never actually talks about angels having wings. Spiritual beings like cherubim and seraphim that do go for the feathered look may have as many as six wings! Can you imagine some guy walking down the street with six wings? It would kind of blow his cover, right?

We don't know what angels might look like as they do their work on earth today. Maybe the girl sitting next to you in math class is an angel on an undercover assignment. Since we can't recognize angels and you wouldn't want to offend a messenger of God, it would be wise to be kind to everyone. It can only make the world a better place.

devotion #16

MIRACLES ARE EVIDENCE

Now while he was in Jerusalem . . . many people saw the miraculous signs he was doing and believed in his name.

— John 2:23

When you read the story of Jesus' life, one thing that jumps out at you is how many miracles he did. People who saw these things were astonished. This man was clearly no ordinary man, and many people believed that he was the Son of God. In fact, Jesus' enemies complained, "Here is this man performing many miraculous signs. If we let him go on like this, *everyone* will believe in him." They knew that miracles were strong evidence that Jesus had divine power.

And miracles didn't only happen in Bible days. God *still* answers prayers

when Christians pray to him in Jesus' name. He still does miracles today: big ones that make you go "Wow!" and small everyday ones. Stop and think about some prayer God answered for your family. You've probably even forgotten some of them. Ask your parents or grandparents to remind you.

People pray for lots of *little* things every day, and time and again God answers! The problem is that by the time God answers the prayer, people have often forgotten that they prayed for it. We don't always recognize when God does something for us. You know how you take it for granted when your mom and dad do things for you? Well, God does lots of stuff for you too. So pay attention and thank him whenever you can.

Jesus did miracles, and those miracles proved his love and power. Although he isn't walking around on earth today, his power to do miracles is still here. He still answers our prayers today.

devotion #17

BEING BORN AGAIN

Jesus declared, "I tell you the truth, no one can see the kingdom of God unless he is born again."

—John 3:3

Ever wonder where the term *born again* came from? One night an old, white-bearded teacher named Nicodemus came to Jesus. Nick nearly fell over backward when Jesus told him that the only way to enter God's kingdom was to be born again. Nick asked if Jesus meant he had to enter a second time into his mother's womb to be born. Jesus explained, "Flesh gives birth to flesh, but the Spirit gives birth to spirit."

See, you've already been born physically. A physical birth lands you in this world, screaming your lungs out. In case no one ever told you, that's what the cake and candles and presents are all about each year. That's a good start, but it isn't enough. You also need to be born spiritually. You may ask, "But how do I do that? How do I become born *again?*"

Here's how it happens: When you believe in Jesus, the Holy Spirit enters your heart to give life to your spirit. God's Spirit gives you life — *eternal* life, in fact — and you've just been born again! You've become one of God's own kids. Sound terrific? Why would God do such a fantastic thing? He does it because he loves you.

Do you want to live forever in God's kingdom? Pray for Jesus to forgive you and ask the Holy Spirit to come into your heart. Then you'll have eternal life. That's what being born again is about.

devotion #18

ON YOUR MARK, GET SET, GO!

The beginning of the gospel about Jesus Christ, the Son of God.

— Mark 1:1

There are four gospels in the Bible — Matthew, Mark, Luke, and John. All of the gospels are good for everybody to read, but here's an interesting point about the gospel of Mark: Bible scholars believe that Mark's gospel was originally written for the Romans. The Romans loved *action*, so Mark included mostly action in his book and hardly any parables or sermons or prayers.

Your youth leader just told you to read the Bible. Your dad agrees. Your mom says there is lots of good stuff for you to learn about. Ready?

Set? But where do you start? It can be pretty overwhelming!

Maybe you think it would be best to just flip it open and read whatever you point to first. So you turn to Leviticus 13:47 and read, " 'If any clothing is contaminated with mildew — any woolen or linen clothing . . . ' " You close your Bible and then open it to 1 Chronicles 1:40 and read, "The sons of Shobal: Alvan, Manahath, Ebal, Shepho and Onam." You close your Bible again, and by now you're probably ready to *keep* it closed and go watch TV.

Listen guys, skip all the deep Bible stuff for now and start with the gospels. And if you *really* want a high-energy read, start with the gospel of Mark. When Mark talks about what Jesus did, he uses a lot of fast-paced words like *immediately*, *at once*, and *quickly*. Mark also describes the action in colorful detail. Mark wrote his gospel for people who like *doing* stuff and just want to know what happened. That makes it a great book for boys.

If you've never read any gospel story from beginning to end, start reading Mark today. Once you've read Mark, then you can read the other stuff. On your Mark, get set, go!

Devotion #19

GOD IS STILL IN BUSINESS

"If the LORD is with us, why has all this happened to us? Where are all his wonders that our fathers told us about when they said, 'Did not the LORD bring us up out of Egypt?' "

— Judges 6:13

When Gideon was a kid, his dad and granddad told him all of the Bible stories about God striking Egypt with plagues. They told him about God parting the Red Sea so the Israelites could escape. But in this Bible passage, Gideon was grown up, and raiders had invaded Israel and were stealing everything in sight. The Israelites had fled their homes and hidden out in caves. Gideon needed a miracle in *his* day.

When things are tough, you may ask the same questions Gideon did. The Bible talks about God doing miracles. So what happened? Why doesn't he still do miracles today? Well, God still does perform miracles. In Gideon's case, God didn't take over and do all the work. He ordered Gideon to fight the raiders. Sure, God did a miracle — the part Gideon couldn't do — but Gideon had to do the part he could do.

God still cares and still performs miracles right now in the twenty-first century. He can heal diseases. He can supply the money you need. In many cases, God will probably ask you to do *your* part — just like he asked Gideon. God expects you to go to the doctor or to do what you can to earn money, but then he does the part you can't do.

Miracles aren't just things of the past. Miracles don't just happen in the pages of Bible storybooks. God is still in the miracle business.

devotion #20

AMAZING WAYS THROUGH THE MAZE

In all your ways acknowledge him, and he will make your paths straight.

— Proverbs 3:6

The Bible tells us to acknowledge God in everything we do. What does *acknowledge* mean? It means making an effort to recognize God, to be aware that he's God, that he's powerful and wise, and that you need his help. Acknowledge God and he'll make your paths straightforward and easier.

When you're trying to figure out the maze on the back of a cereal box, there's nothing straight about it. It goes this way and that way, backward, up and down, and all over the place. Or maybe you've wandered through a corn maze. Sure, it starts out as fun, but when you do a thousand-acre maze, you get good and lost. The whole idea of a maze is to make it hard for you to find the path. Life can be like that. Maybe you feel your whole life is one big maze. What do you do?

Well, if you were lost in a corn maze, you'd holler, right? So holler. Call out to God. Pray. If you pray when you're faced with a choice, God will make your paths straight. You'll still make a few wrong turns from time to time, but overall your way will be easier without twenty dozen false leads and dead ends. God can help get you where you should be.

God has a bird's eye view of things on earth, and if you're talking to him, he can help you find amazing ways through the maze.

devotion #21

HE WHO WORSHIPS GOD, WINS!

Jesus said to him, "Away from me, Satan! For it is written, 'Worship the Lord your God, and serve him only.' "

— Matthew 4:10

One day the devil tried to tempt Jesus. He showed Jesus all the kingdoms of this world and their glittering splendor and fabulous riches. The devil said, "All this I will give you . . . if you will bow down and worship me" (Matthew 4:9). Jesus told Satan to get away, and then he quoted Scripture, saying that we are to worship God instead — and *only* God.

The devil doesn't usually come out so bold. Usually he's happy if he can just get you to worship your

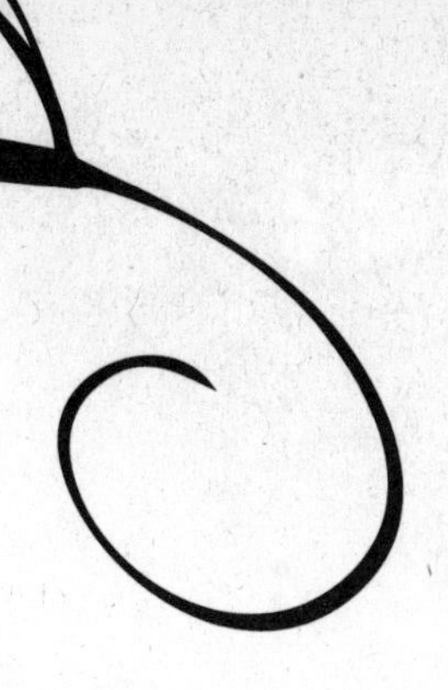

belongings and your toys — anything but God. See, Jesus said that the first and greatest commandment was to love God with all your heart, but a lot of people think the number one rule is to get as many toys as they can just to enjoy life. Their motto is, "He who has the most toys when he dies, wins." Wrong!

The Bible says that greed is just like idol worship (Colossians 3:5). Now, there's nothing wrong with having toys or fancy new gadgets. It's okay to like them and think they're cool and take good care of them. But the problem is if you obsess over your stuff or put material things before God. Then it becomes like idol worship — like you are worshiping a thing instead of God.

Enjoy the toys and things that God has given you. Just remember that God is the one who gives you cool stuff to enjoy — so make God number one in your life.

Devotion #22

LETTING GOD DEAL WITH THINGS

Do not take revenge, my friends . . . for it is written: "It is mine to avenge; I will repay," says the Lord.

— Romans 12:19

Paul was talking to Christians at Rome who had been persecuted for their faith. Paul knew that these Christians were only human. He knew that they must have felt like getting back at people who were accusing them and hassling them and spitting on them and cursing them. But Paul told them to let God be the one to avenge them. That meant really trusting God.

You probably know the feeling. When your sister kicks you, you probably really want to slug her in return. But if you do, your dad hears the ruckus,

walks in, and gives you *both* a time out. If you can't work it out with your sister, ask for your dad or mom's help. Rather than hitting your sister back, the best solution might be to tell your dad and let *him* deal with her. Then you're out of the picture. Dad doesn't have to punish you for slugging her, because you didn't.

God is like your dad — only he sees *everything*, knows *exactly* what happened, and can deal with things better. God can make sure that people are paid back for the evil they do, so Christians shouldn't take the law into their own hands. Besides, what if God *changes* that person into a better person instead of punishing him? He often does. So don't get in God's way.

Don't take revenge on those who persecute or hassle you. If God wants to punish people or change them, stand back and let him. In the meantime, pray for your enemies.

devotion #23

LIVING LIKE PHANTOMS

"Each man's life is but a breath. Man is a mere phantom as he goes to and fro: He bustles about, but only in vain."

— Psalm 39:5–6

When the Bible talks about people being like phantoms, it doesn't mean they fly through walls — unless they do a major wipeout on their skateboard. It means that they're busy and on the go, but they never accomplish anything. They're just a bunch of hot air. Their entire life is like a balloon shooting around the room with air squealing out of it. They live in vain, meaning for nothing.

Ever wished you were a ghost so you could walk through walls, fly through the air, and maybe scare people?

Okay, scaring people is no fun for *them*, but the fact is, mankind has always wanted to fly. These days, you can get on a plane and do that. For most kids, the closest they come to flying is taking a ride in the Salt & Pepper Shaker at the amusement park.

Flying is fun, but you *don't* want to live your life like a phantom the way some people do. They bustle about — run around making a lot of noise — but their life never actually makes a difference. They never help others. If you want a *real* life that counts, love God and others. Not only will it make life better right now, but God will reward you for it in heaven.

If you don't want to live a fleeting, phantom life, then make sure to love God and others. That way, you can live a life that really counts.

devotion #24

HOW THE UNIVERSE WAS FORMED

By faith we understand that the universe was formed at God's command, so that what is seen was not made out of what was visible.

— Hebrews 11:3

In the time before time, there were no planets, no asteroids, not even one speck of space dust. There was no light and no energy — not even enough to recharge one tiny triple-A battery. There was nothing but God. Then God gave the command, and the whole universe came into being. And get this! He created the *entire universe* out of nothing.

Have you ever looked at the moon through a pair of binoculars, peeked at Mars through a telescope, or been on a field trip to a planetarium? You probably have a hint of an idea of how big our galaxy is. Just the small piece of God's creation that we can observe is amazing, but the universe includes millions of galaxies like ours.

No humans were around when the universe was formed. Since we didn't observe its creation ourselves, we have to have faith to believe what we don't understand. We have God's Word telling us that the universe was formed at his command. But we can also observe the amazing complexity of the universe. Just look around and study science to see that a loving Creator put tremendous thought into everything, from the greatest galaxy to the smallest DNA.

Unbelievers think that the earth and everything in the galaxy formed by accident. It takes faith to believe that God created the universe, but guys, it takes a whole lot *more* faith to believe that everything created itself without God's help.

devotion #25

CHURCH – BELIEVERS BELONG TOGETHER

Let us not give up meeting together,
as some are in the habit of doing,
but let us encourage one another.
— Hebrews 10:25

In the early church, believers were sometimes persecuted for being Christians. It could be dangerous to meet. All it took was one spy and you could all get arrested. But often things weren't so serious. A lot of people stopped attending meetings because they simply couldn't be bothered to go. They skipped so many services that they got in the habit of not going to church.

Okay, if there's such a howling blizzard outside your door that the dog teams are freezing solid and even the

penguins are falling over dead from frostbite, that's one thing. Or if your family is colonizing Mars, you can't zip back once a week to your hometown church. But hey, if your *only* reason for not going to church is because you want to sleep in or you just don't feel like going, that really doesn't cut it.

Sure, you can be a Christian all alone, but that's not God's plan. God made people to need other people — to belong to a community. It's important for Christians to go to church. It strengthens you when you spend time with other believers, because you encourage each other. Worshiping with others inspires you. And your teachers have prepared important lessons from God's Word to teach you.

You won't always feel like going to church, but meeting with other Christians is a good habit to get into. So dig your dog team out of the snowdrifts, jump in the sled, and go.

Devotion #26

DEALING WITH PERSECUTION

"Blessed are you when men hate you, when they exclude you and insult you . . . because of the Son of Man. Rejoice in that day and leap for joy, because great is your reward in heaven."

— Luke 6:22 – 23

Jesus knew that Christians would be persecuted for believing in him. There would be times when people would mock and insult them. Sometimes their former friends would snub them. So how are Christians supposed to deal with this kind of rejection? Jesus gave a surprising answer. He said that we were supposed to rejoice and be happy about it.

You're probably thinking that no way do you feel happy when kids tease you for believing in Jesus or for going to church. And you're *not* particularly glad when old pals don't hang around with you anymore because you stand up for what's right. Being cut from the herd can hurt. So how do you deal with it? And what about all this is supposed to make you happy?

First of all, you know you're being rejected or insulted because you're making God happy, and that ought to make *you* happy. And what should make you even happier is the knowledge that God has promised to bless you for standing up for Jesus. God is going to see to it that you receive a *great* reward in heaven for your troubles down here.

Leap for joy when other kids insult you? Hey, if you don't wanna leap, at least smile. Your future is very, very bright and blessed.

Devotion #27

CHOOSE COOL WATER, NOT DUST

"They have forsaken me, the spring of living water, and have dug their own cisterns, broken cisterns that cannot hold water."

— Jeremiah 2:13

Israel was a very dry land. It didn't rain much. So if you had a spring where water gushed out of the ground, you were happy. The Gihon Spring supplied water for all Jerusalem, but other cities had wells. When the well went dry, the people had to drink water from underground tanks called cisterns. It was bad enough that the water tasted stale, but if the cistern had a leak, there was nothing there! God says in this verse that his people have turned away from him, the living

water, and have chosen to worship false gods, which is like choosing to drink from a broken cistern.

Now, who in his right mind would trade something great for something broken? It'd be like if you had a brand new Xbox — the box, the controls, the game CDs, the works — and some kid came along and talked you into trading that for his old, broken setup. Would that be smart? No. So why would anyone make a trade like that?

They'd do it if they were *tricked* into it. Like, if the kid stuffed his old game inside a brand-new box and promised that it was new and worked great. When people forsake God and choose false religions or put their trust in other things, they think they're getting something new and better, but they're only getting ripped off.

Have you opened up the box of Christian faith and tried out the real deal? If you've experienced the genuine Jesus, you won't trade him for a cheap imitation.

devotion #28

MONSTERS IN THE CLOSET? NAH!

I will lie down and sleep in peace, for you alone, O LORD, make me dwell in safety.

— Psalm 4:8

Even believers thousands of years ago sometimes got afraid at night—which was why God promised that when they lay down in bed, they wouldn't be afraid and their sleep would be sweet. Sounds great, but how do you make it work for *you*? You can lock your door, sure, and turn on a night-light, but a big way to not fear is to remember the promises in the Bible, keep them in your heart, and quote them when you're afraid.

Like in the movie *Monsters Inc.*, you may sometimes worry that there are monsters in your closet or under the bed. A shadow on the wall can

look scary. It's no fun if you're too scared to sleep, so you huddle under your blankets, sweating. Is your sleep sweet or sweaty? Or maybe *you* don't have problems with that, but one of your friends does. So what's the solution? How do you drive away fear?

Besides obvious stuff like leaving a night-light on, you need to trust God and remind yourself of his Word. Here are some promises to quote when you're fearful: "Even though I walk through the valley of the shadow of death, I will fear *no* evil, for you are with me" (Psalm 23:4). "God is my salvation; I will trust and *not* be afraid" (Isaiah 12:2).

Quoting God's Word is like turning on a spiritual night-light. Remember, if you're a Christian, Jesus is with you, and he's far more powerful than anything. His angels surround your bed.

devotion #29

MYSTERIOUS ANGEL BODYGUARDS

The angel of the LORD
encamps around those who fear him,
and he delivers them.

— Psalm 34:7

One of the jobs God has given angels is to protect humans from physical and spiritual harm. Several times in the Bible, God sent angels to help people. For example, two angels protected Lot and his family by half-leading, half-dragging them out of a doomed city (Genesis 19:10–16).

Many Christians believe that the same angel guards us all the time. Other people say that each believer has *two* guardian angels. These ideas may or may not be true. We don't actually know for certain since the Bible doesn't say. What it *does* say is this: "He will command his angels concerning you to guard you in all your ways" (Psalm 91:11).

What's important to know is that angels are powerful. They are armed and dangerous and — thank goodness! — they're on your side! If you want to find out just how awesome angels are and how scared men get when they see them, read Matthew 28:2–4. The Roman soldiers guarding Jesus' tomb shook so badly they collapsed. Usually angels don't appear in all their power and glory. They know how much it rattles humans.

Since angels are so powerful, it's comforting to know that God loves us and has set them around us to guard us.

Devotion #30

WE WERE THERE. WE SAW IT HAPPEN!

We did not follow cleverly invented stories when we told you about the power and coming of our Lord Jesus Christ, but we were eyewitnesses of his majesty.

— 2 Peter 1:16

Peter left his smelly fishnets to follow Jesus. Peter lived with Jesus for over three years and saw him do astonishing miracles. He was in Jerusalem when Jesus was crucified, and he saw him after he came back to life. So when Peter told people about Jesus' work, if anyone said, "Yeah, sure. Nice story," he insisted, "These aren't cunning, clever, made-up stories! These things *happened*! I *saw* them with my own eyes!"

People in Peter's time were used to hearing invented stories about godlike characters. The Greeks and Romans made up myths about Zeus and Hercules and Jupiter to explain the mysteries of the world. Today, we hear lots of made-up stories in books and movies, with characters like Superman, Hercules, and Spider-Man. They're fun stories, but they are made-up. The people that read Peter's book must have wondered if it was also made-up. But Peter makes it clear that he saw these events with his own eyes.

There are so many creative and interesting stories to read today, but it may be difficult to know the difference between fantasy and fact. Just remember, when it comes to the good news about Jesus, there's nothing made-up about it. The Bible is not a book of fantastic fables like the adventures of Hercules. Witnesses who actually *saw* these things wrote about them in the gospels.

Jesus was a real man. He lived and breathed and walked this earth and did astonishing miracles. He was and is the Son of God.

Devotion #31

TAKING THE PLUNGE

"Repent and be baptized ... And you will receive the gift of the Holy Spirit."

— Acts 2:38

Believing in Jesus saves you, so why do you need to get baptized? Surely the water isn't washing away your sins. No. John the Baptist said to Jesus, "I baptize you with water, but he will baptize you with the Holy Spirit" (Mark 1:8). When you get saved, God's Holy Spirit enters your heart and cleanses you. Baptism is an *outward* symbol of what the Holy Spirit has done and a sign and seal of God's promises.

In the Early Church, Christians were baptized soon after they believed. Maybe you've believed in Jesus for years but you haven't taken the plunge yet. It's definitely something you should do.

Now, different Christian churches have different views on *when* you should be baptized or exactly *how* you should be baptized, but the point is, if you're a believer, you should be baptized.

The apostle Paul also explained that baptism (going under the water) is kind of like dying and being buried. Then, "just as Christ was raised from the dead . . . we too may live a new life" (Romans 6:4). You then rise out of the water to new life. Got that? Just like Jesus died and came back to life, baptism is "death" to your old, selfish life. Bottom line: baptism is a serious, public statement that you've made up your mind to live for Jesus.

Baptism is a serious step. It means turning from your selfish, self-centered ways and going all out for God. If you're a believer, then baptism should be next on your list.

devotion #32

JESUS' RETURN FROM HEAVEN

"Men will see the Son of Man coming in clouds with great power and glory. And he will send his angels and gather his elect from the four winds."

— Mark 13:26–27

Christians have different ideas about what earth's final days will be like. The book of Revelation is deep and mysterious, so we don't understand it all — yet. But one thing Jesus was *very clear* about is that he will return one day. When he comes back in the sky, people all around the planet will see him. For two thousand years, Christians have wanted Jesus to return and end all wars and famines and set up the perfect kingdom of God on earth. Christians living today want the same thing. Or maybe you hope Jesus will *wait* a while. Maybe you want to grow up, graduate high school, and do stuff first. Maybe you don't want this world to end quite yet.

Don't worry. Jesus' kingdom will be a whole lot *more* fun than life right now. It's *not* like we're going to leave earth and then float around on clouds forever. Some Christians think that after taking us to heaven for a wonderful time with him and all the Christians who have ever lived, we'll return to earth. Then, instead of selfish, greedy people running the place, there will be love, peace, and harmony on earth.

We don't know all the details of Jesus' return. But we do know that he is coming back one day with power and great glory, and that life will be better than it's ever been.

devotion #33

GOD – ALWAYS MERCIFUL AND LOVING

Who is a God like you, who pardons sin and forgives the transgression? . . . You do not stay angry forever but delight to show mercy.

— Micah 7:18

Micah was a prophet of God, and he lived back when the tough Law of Moses was the law of the land. This was long before Jesus was born. Yet when Micah described God, he didn't talk about an angry God who loved to judge people when they goofed up. Micah said that God would rather forgive sin; he said God loved to show mercy.

Sometimes you might wonder, "Why was God mean and angry in the olden days, yet so loving and kind and

forgiving after Jesus came?" Or maybe you've heard unbelievers ask, "Why did God destroy cities and judge nations in the past, yet when Jesus came along, he hugged little children and told us to love our enemies?" Why the change?

No change. God hasn't changed. God judged nations in the past because they rebelled against him, persecuted God's people, and did other bad things. And the news is: God still judges nations today. But God is not *only* into judgment and justice, he's also big on love. Even back in the olden days, he delighted to forgive people.

God was forgiving and loving and merciful in the past, and he still is today. God said, "I the Lord do not change" (Malachi 3:6). God has always wanted to forgive.

devotion #34

HELPING YOUR FAITH GROW

Faith comes from hearing the message, and the message is heard through the word of Christ.

— Romans 10:17

When you read the gospels or hear your pastor talk about Jesus and God's Spirit opens your eyes to all the amazing stuff Jesus said and did, you just *know* that Jesus was one of a kind. No one else taught the amazing things he taught or did the miracles he did. And certainly no one else died and came back to life! And once you put your faith in Jesus and trust him to save you, you have eternal life.

But even after you believe in Jesus, your faith is still tested. Like maybe you're confused or afraid.

Or maybe you're going through a difficult time. Maybe everything seems hopeless and you just need some hope to hang onto so you don't sink in the "quicksand of gloom."

Where do you get your hope? What helps you believe that God is with you and that things will turn out?

You get that hope and inspiration the same way you received it in the first place — by listening to the truth about Jesus and by sitting down and opening up your Bible and reading it. Are you worried about some problem? Are you afraid? Do you wonder where God is when you need him? Do you feel mentally wiped out?

If you want your faith to grow stronger, read God's Word. That's where your spiritual strength comes from. Plug in to God and recharge your batteries today.

devotion #35

DESPERATELY THIRSTY DUDES

O God, you are my God, earnestly I seek you; my soul thirsts for you . . . in a dry and weary land where there is no water.

— Psalm 63:1

Before David became king, the army of old King Saul chased David all around the deserts of Judah. David wanted a cool, refreshing drink and longed to relax in the shade, but it wasn't safe to camp near a well. He had to stay out in dry, dusty, dangerous places. That's when it dawned on him that he needed God just as much as water.

Have you ever been "dying of thirst"? Ever been on an all-day hike when everyone forgot to bring water? Or ever staggered up to a soda pop machine, nearly wild with thirst, and then realize that you have no change? Being thirsty doesn't just mean you *want* a drink. "Thirsty" gets to the point where cool liquid is all you can think of. Doctors say that people should glug down about six to eight glasses of water a day to stay healthy. We often don't do that, so we get sick, have headaches, etc.

It's the same with our relationship with God. We should tank up on God's Spirit. But what do we do instead? We skip prayer time, miss Bible reading, and end up weak and confused. David was thirsty for God, and we are too: we just need to realize it.

Feel a thirst for God? Don't stagger around a dusty desert like a thirsty camel. Make a run for God's well, let down the bucket, and have a good, cool drink.

devotion #36

PUBLIC, UNITED WORSHIP

In the great assembly
I will praise the LORD.

— Psalm 26:12

To *assemble* means to gather people together — so an *assembly* is a gathering of people. You know, like an assembly in your school gymnasium. So what's David saying? He's saying that it's great for a group of God's people to get together to glorify God. Back in King David's day, God's people assembled in a big old tent called the sanctuary.

Maybe you're one of those kids who wonder why on earth Christians have to all gather in church and praise God together? Why can't you just praise God alone at home while ... um, playing a video game or building

something out of Lego bricks? Well, there's a reason. The Bible actually *tells* believers to get together, focus on him together, and praise him out loud. The only reason *not* to would be if you were out of breath and basically dead.

And speaking of Lego . . . Think about putting together a bunch of little pieces. The scattered pieces may not look like much by themselves, but once you *assemble* them into one big object, then they look cool. That's why a Christian assembly is cool to God. It looks great to him, and it sounds great. And there is another thing: worshiping God inspires and strengthens Christians.

You may not understand why united worship is important now, but at least respect God and others by not zoning out or talking. When you're in church, do your best to focus on God. You can always play later.

Devotion #37

FEAR CAN BE A GOOD THING

The fear of the LORD is pure,
enduring forever.

— Psalm 19:9

The Bible often tells us to fear God. You may ask, "If God is love, why should I fear him? Isn't he on my side?" Yes, he is. But fear is sometimes a good thing. True, a lot of fear is just worry and fretting — like being afraid of the dentist or fearing that World War III will start. But some fear is worthwhile. Since the fear of the Lord is *pure*, you know it's a good thing.

You should be afraid of some things. For example, if you're afraid to climb up on top of some steel tower during a thunderstorm and get deliberately struck by a billion volts of lightning, that's a *good* fear. It shows that you're thinking.

It shows that you're aware of the power of a lightning bolt and how badly it can fry your molecules. You respect it. That's what the "fear of the Lord" is about: being in awe of God's power.

"Yeah," you say, "but God is *love*. Lightning is not love." True, but who invented lightning? *God.* In his Narnia books, C. S. Lewis tells readers that the lion Aslan "is not a tame lion." Aslan can be gentle, but he's also powerful and dangerous. God is like that. You don't mess around with him. He's not a jolly, roly-poly Santa Claus. He's God.

The fear of the Lord is not a bad thing. It's a positive thing. It's pure. When you begin to fear God, it shows you've started to understand who God is and how powerful he is.

devotion #38

HIDING GOD'S WORD DOWN DEEP

I have hidden your word in my heart
that I might not sin against you.
— Psalm 119:11

When this verse talks about hiding God's Word in your heart, it doesn't mean stashing it somewhere so little kids can't find it. When it says to "hide" it, the verse means getting the Bible *so* deep down in your mind that it's almost part of you. And it's not only talking about memorizing Bible verses, but also about tuning in to them. Do that and you're a lot less likely to sin against God.

If you have to make a decision and wonder what to do, it sure makes it a lot easier if a verse from the Bible suddenly comes to mind, telling you exactly what God thinks of your plans, right?

Since you don't always have a Bible handy, plant some verses in your mind. Get them deep in your heart. And how do you do *that*?

Well, just like you have to memorize multiplication tables or lines from a play, you should memorize important verses from the Bible. Some people only have to read a verse a few times and it sticks. Good for them! But most of us, if we want to write it onto our brain's hard drive, have to actually memorize it. Do that. Then the Holy Spirit can remind you of it when you need direction the most.

If you can't remember what God's Word says, it's easy to sin and do wrong things. If you know what the Bible says, it's a whole lot easier to make the right choice.

Devotion #39

DON'T JUST WAIL! PRAY!

They were at their wits' end. Then they cried out to the LORD in their trouble, and he brought them out of their distress.

— Psalm 107:27–28

One day a merchant ship was sailing along — la di da — when a terrible storm hit. Monster waves lifted the ship high into the sky then hurled it down into the depths. Then up again, then down again. The storm was so wild, the sailors staggered around the deck like drunken men. They were out of their minds with fear. They began praying! Oh yeah, they prayed! And God answered. He stilled the storm to a whisper, and they reached port safe and sound.

Have *you* ever been at your wits' end? Maybe you're not staggering and sliding all over the deck of a ship, but have you ever been in danger? Have you ever been afraid? Or have you ever lost something — like your homework or some friend's toy — and you desperately needed to find it? What do you do? Do you cry out to God?

God says, "You will seek me and find me when you seek me with all your heart" (Jeremiah 29:13). That's a promise. Only make sure you're actually praying with all your heart and not just lying on your bed moaning and wailing. God said about the ancient Israelites, "They do not cry out to me from their hearts but wail upon their beds" (Hosea 7:14).

When you're at your wits' end, don't just wail. Cry out to God. He'll deliver you. He'll help you when no one else can, but it might not be in the way you expect.

Devotion #40

TROPHIES WAITING IN HEAVEN

Everyone who competes in the games goes into strict training. They do it to get a crown that will not last; but we do it to get a crown that will last forever.

— 1 Corinthians 9:25

When ancient Greek athletes won a competition, they didn't get gold medals. They got to wear a crown made of leaves, usually branches of laurel leaves, olive leaves, or pine needles. Obviously, those things didn't last. Pine needles stay green the longest, but after a while even *they* dry up. Even Christmas trees eventually have to get chucked.

These days when you win a track and field event, you probably get one of those colored ribbons. It shows that you

accomplished something, but unless you pin it to your bedroom wall, it can get lost really quickly. Now a shiny metal trophy is different. Usually that's bigger and not so easy to lose — although, with the disasters that some kids' rooms are, they could lose even *that*.

Paul said that the treasures of this life were like leafy crowns, wilting like yesterday's salad. As Christians, we're out to earn treasures that will last forever. And the good thing is, you can't lose these rewards no matter how messy your room is, 'cause they're not on earth. God holds onto them for you. "He has given us . . . an inheritance that can never perish, spoil or fade — kept in heaven for you" (1 Peter 1:3 – 4).

When you get to heaven, you'll inherit all the treasures and awards God has been keeping for you. Your whole life of serving God will be rewarded.

devotion #41

FANTASTIC OUTER SPACE

When I consider your heavens . . . the moon and the stars, which you have set in place, what is man that you are mindful of him, the son of man that you care for him?

— Psalm 8:3–4

King David, who wrote this psalm, must've loved to climb up on his flat palace roof at night and look up at the moon and the zillion stars stretched out over Jerusalem. Maybe he took his kids up with him, lay on his back, and pointed out the planets and constellations. David was in awe. When he thought about how vast the universe was, he was amazed that God cared so much for people here on earth.

Think about it: David didn't even know a hundredth of what we know today! Back then people only had their eyeballs. Today we have telescopes staring into distant galaxies. We have satellites shooting past the moons of Jupiter taking snapshots of their ice canyons. We can study photos of dust storms ripping across the deserts of Mars and download color photos of stars exploding.

The miracle is that even with all the endless galaxies stuffed with mysterious stars stretching out to infinity, God cares for us! What is it about people that God's mind is full of us? Why can't he just stop thinking about us? Well, he loves us, that's why! And why? People are his special creation.

It's awesome to stare out into space at the universe that God created, but it's even more awesome to realize how much he cares for you.

devotion #42

GOD IS YOUR DAD

Because you are sons, God sent the Spirit of his Son into our hearts, the Spirit who calls out, "Abba, Father."

— Galatians 4:6

Jesus is God's Son. We are not God's sons and daughters by birth. But when you believe in Jesus and ask him to come into your life, God *adopts* you and makes you his child. He sends the Spirit of his Son, Jesus, to live in your heart. Now, maybe it doesn't come naturally to you to think of God as your dad, but it's perfectly natural for Jesus, so his Spirit in you calls out, "Abba, Father!"

When you talk to your dad, do you normally call him "Father"?

Probably not. Chances are you call him *dad*. Well, that's what *Abba* means. *Abba* isn't an English word, as you probably guessed. It's an ancient Aramaic word, and it's like saying, "dad." The whole idea is that you can have a close, warm relationship with God, just like with a dad.

Jesus talked about this once. He told a bunch of dads one day: "Which of you, if his son asks for bread, will give him a stone? If you . . . know how to give good gifts to your children, how much more will your Father in heaven give good gifts to those who ask him!" (Matthew 7:9–11). God is your dad. He loves you and wants the best for you.

Do you want a close relationship with God? Do you want him to adopt you as one of his own kids? Then believe in Jesus, and you'll be one of God's adopted children too!

devotion #43

GO WHERE YOU MEAN TO GO

Do not conform any longer to the pattern of this world, but be transformed by the renewing of your mind.

— Romans 12:2

If you're a Christian, you're a changed person. Once Jesus has saved you, your old ways of thinking begin to get replaced. God sends his Spirit into your heart and starts changing you by giving your mind a new outlook. He knows you'll be tempted to flip back to acting like those who haven't been changed by Jesus, so he warns, "from now on don't conform to your old ways."

Have you ever started to go somewhere in your house, and then you got distracted? You hop off your bed,

walk down the hall, and . . . wander into the kitchen. You look around and wonder, "Huh? Why did I come here?" You weren't even hungry, but you just walked to Grand Snack Central out of habit. You were following the old programming, the old pattern. If you want to go to where you really mean to go, you need to remember you have a *new* direction — then head there.

When God comes into your life, he begins changing you immediately. You go to do something stupid and realize, "Whoa! I don't want to do *that* anymore!" So you stop. Sometimes the changes are big and fast. Other times it takes a while to stop mindlessly repeating old habits. It takes time to replace old habits with new habits.

It can be easy to flip back to your old way of thinking. So make an effort to stop that and to let God's Spirit transform your thought patterns.

Devotion #44

REWARD DAY FOR CHRISTIANS

We must all appear before the judgment seat of Christ, that each one may receive what is due him for the things done while in the body, whether good or bad.

— 2 Corinthians 5:10

When you believe in Jesus, he gives you eternal life, and he prepares a fantastic place in heaven for you. But before you move into your home in paradise, you'll be required to show up at the judgment seat of Christ. Jesus will be your judge, and he'll examine everything you have ever done or said in your entire life.

Maybe you thought that after you left this world, you shot straight into heaven, ran up and down the streets of gold, moved into your new mansion, and maybe took off for a vacation to the moons of Jupiter? After all, all your sins have been forgiven, right? Right, they have. But before you do anything else, you'll have a serious, one-on-one appointment with Jesus Christ.

This is not to judge whether you go to heaven or not. If you love Jesus and have tried to do what he says, your destination's already settled. This session is to gloriously reward you for all the good you've ever done and to burn away all the garbage you collected in your life. You'll be so happy about all the good you did, but crying about your selfish, bad deeds. Then Jesus will wipe all tears from your eyes.

Knowing that you'll appear before the judgment seat of Christ one day should remind you that what you do in this life really counts.

devotion #45

WARS ON THE EVENING NEWS

"You will hear of wars and rumors of wars, but see to it that you are not alarmed. Such things must happen, but the end is still to come."

— Matthew 24:6

Jesus' disciples had just finished asking, "What will be the sign of your coming, and of the end of the age?" Jesus told them what to look for, but part of his answer was telling them what *not* to get worried about. "You'll hear about wars. Don't get alarmed. You'll hear that a war might start. Don't freak out. Wars are bad, but they're not necessarily the end of the world."

These days, with newspeople reporting right from war zones and blown-up cars smoking all over your TV screen, it may feel like the war is happening in your living room. You've heard that one day the Battle of Armageddon will mean the end of the world, so maybe you get worried that some new battle you see on TV is going to start it. Or maybe you see some guy carrying signs that read: "Armageddon has begun!"

It's natural to worry, but don't. Don't lose sleep over it. Jesus specifically said not to be alarmed. He wants us to be comforted by the knowledge that no matter what happens, God is in control and we are in his hands. Wars have been happening since the beginning of civilization. Jesus told us that these things must happen. War is serious business, and lots of people suffer in wars. So pray for the people involved.

Jesus knows that people often worry when serious stuff is happening, and that's why he warned *us not* to worry or get alarmed.

Devotion #46

LOTS OF PEOPLE SINGING

Sing to the LORD a new song, his praise in the assembly of the saints.

— Psalm 149:1

King David loved worshiping God with music. David was a musician and wrote lots of new hymns called psalms. People started singing his songs in the "assembly of the saints," the gatherings of believers. David even played instruments to praise God! (No, he did not play the electric guitar.) Clearly, David loved music.

Now, some kids today like singing; others don't. Maybe you like listening to music on your iPod or singing retro tunes. But when everybody's in church singing together from the hymnbook or the words projected on the overhead

screen, you might wonder, "Why are we *doing* this? Does God actually like hearing all of us sing?"

Yes, he does. That's why the Bible says for believers to sing together. It can be a powerful experience. Think about the theme song from your favorite TV show. What if the creator of the show came to town and you and a hundred other kids were all belting out that song? That'd be fun, huh? Well, the Creator of the universe is in church, so sing wholeheartedly for him too.

Whether your church is singing an old hymn like "Amazing Grace" or a new song someone just wrote, join in. You may not always feel like singing, but God is definitely worthy of praise.

Devotion #47

AVOIDING THE DARK SIDE

The sacrifices of pagans are offered to demons, not to God, and I do not want you to be participants with demons.

—1 Corinthians 10:20

Back in Roman days, pagans (idol worshipers) sacrificed animals to the idols of their gods and then ate the meat of the sacrifice. It was part of their pagan worship. Most people couldn't afford meat often, so this was a special reward for worshiping Hercules or the other gods. Often they made the event into a feast and invited their friends—including Christian friends. Paul warned Christian believers not to eat that meat. It was like taking part in idol worship.

This principle applies today too. Not that you're going to be tempted to eat a Hercules steak or food dedicated to demons. Think of other stuff that might tempt you. For example, a non-Christian friend may invite you to his house after school to play an adults-only video game. Now, that game may be exciting to play, but it's so evil that it will seriously mess up your mind. Don't participate in it.

The same principle applies to music, videos, comic books, or whatever. There are *good* videos, *good* music, and *good* comic books, but if something is dark and demonic — or if it glorifies violence — then steer clear of it. It will influence you in the wrong direction. Besides, it'll end up giving you nightmares.

There are enough clean books, games, and movies available that it should be pretty easy to find good, fun stuff to do. So stay away from the dark side.

devotion #48

LOOKS JUST LIKE HIS DAD

"Anyone who has seen me has seen the Father. How can you say, 'Show us the Father'?"
— John 14:9

Jesus' disciples knew that he was God's Son, but they wanted Jesus to show them his Father. They wanted to see God. Um . . . guys, listen, that's a bit of a problem. God the Father is invisible. You *can't* see him. But fortunately, Jesus is the "image of the invisible God" (Colossians 1:15). That's why, when God decided to give people a clear idea of what he was like, he sent his Son, Jesus, to live on earth as a man.

Maybe you wish *you* could see God. Actually, even if you could, it's not such a great idea. There's a *reason* God made himself invisible. God's so

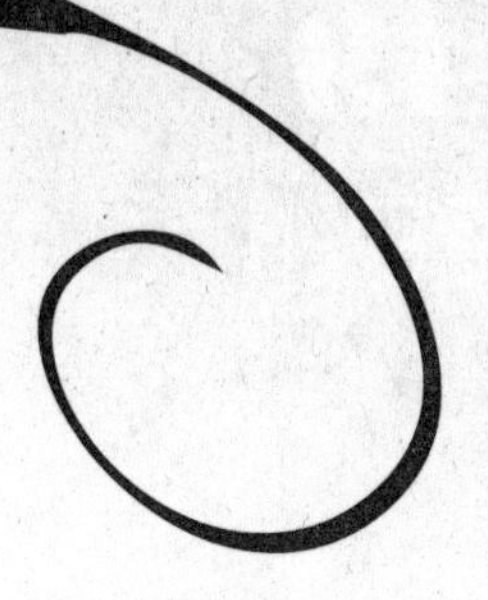

powerful that if you look directly at his face, you'll fall over dead. God told Moses, "You cannot see my face, for no one may see me and live" (Exodus 33:20). It'd be like lying down on a launching pad under a rocket so you can get a good, close look at its engines firing up. It's just *not* a good idea.

You're best looking at Jesus. But you say, "How can I? He's not on earth anymore." Listen, knowing what Jesus is like does not mean seeing how big his nose is, what color his hair is, or if his eyes get crinkle lines when he smiles. That's not the important stuff. In fact, the gospels don't even describe how he looks. What's truly important is who Jesus *was* and how he lived!

If you want to see God, look at Jesus. And if you want to get a good look at Jesus, read all about his amazing life in the gospels.

devotion #49

WAR IN THE SPIRITUAL REALM

Then the LORD opened the servant's eyes, and he looked and saw the hills full of horses and chariots of fire all around Elisha.

— 2 Kings 6:17

Once the prophet Elisha was in a city, and the king of Aram sent an army to capture him. When Elisha's servant woke up the next morning, he saw hundreds of Aramean soldiers with horses and chariots around the city. (Bet that really woke him up!) "What shall we *do*?" he wailed. Elisha prayed, "O Lord, open his eyes so he may see." That's when the servant guy saw the hills full of fiery chariots and blazing horses—these angels outnumbered the king's army.

Just because you can't see something, it doesn't mean it's not there.

Think about it. Armies usually like to stay hidden and out of sight if they can. That's why Robin Hood's merry men wore green clothes — so they could hide in Sherwood Forest and not be spotted. That's why stealth aircraft use radar-absorbing paint and other technology to make them nearly invisible. Angels perfected stealth stuff over 4,000 years ago.

We often imagine one or two guardian angels protecting us, and maybe that's usually the case. But obviously there are times when God sends entire armies of angels to defend his people. That's when there's a huge battle happening in the spiritual realm. Think about that the next time there's trouble in your city or on the news.

God didn't leave us here alone without protection. He has sent his angels to guard us, and when things get serious, he sends out whole armies of angels.

devotion #50

WHY GOD GIVES US GIFTS

There are different kinds of gifts, but the same Spirit. . . . Now to each one the manifestation of the Spirit is given for the common good.

—1 Corinthians 12:4, 7

When the Spirit of God lives in your heart, he gives you power to live the Christian faith. But he *also* gives you some unique "gifts." These gifts are abilities and spiritual talents, and they're different for each person. But the reason is always the same—to help you and others.

Ever wanted to have special powers—like miraculous powers? Well, we humans can't do miracles. But God can! Sometimes he gives people gifts of insight, knowledge, or ability. If that happens, it's not some power you have. God's Spirit is the one who does it. If you could do it on demand, you'd be tempted to use it for *selfish* reasons . . . like kids in the movies do.

God's Spirit gives Christians all kinds of spiritual gifts. Sometimes he gives believers the gift of knowing what others are going through so they can pray for them or encourage them. Maybe God will give you the gift of wisdom or the gift of knowledge. You'll know something that you had no way of finding out. Or maybe your spiritual gift will be something totally different. It might take time for your gift to show up, but it *will* show up.

Just remember: God doesn't let you do cool stuff to make you look great. That's not the way God operates. He does it to help *you* and to help *others*.

devotion #51

FIGHTING BEASTS OR BEASTLY FEASTS

If I fought wild beasts in Ephesus for merely human reasons, what have I gained? If the dead are not raised, "Let us eat and drink, for tomorrow we die."

— 1 Corinthians 15:32

In Roman days, criminals were thrown to the lions in the arena. Sometimes the guys were given weapons to give them a fighting chance. Paul talked about the danger he had faced for the sake of the gospel, saying it was like he had fought wild beasts. The Bible doesn't say Paul got into an arena to fight actual lions with a sword and a net. This verse is symbolic.

Paul didn't want to do that major fighting for no reason. He was doing it because he understood resurrection through Christ. If there is nothing for us after death—no reward for doing good, no punishment for doing bad—then why try to do good? What's the point in fighting temptation and bad habits? You might as well sit around eating pizza and drinking soda pop all day. If there is no purpose to life, why not live like a slob, never clean your room, and never lift a finger to help? A lot of people think that way.

They're wrong. The Bible puts us on notice that every human being who has ever lived on this planet will be raised from the dead one day and rewarded or punished for how they lived. If you love God and believe in Jesus, you'll be raised to everlasting life. That's true, but guess what? You'll *also* be rewarded in heaven for how *well* you obeyed God.

It's worth it to battle wild beasts—temptations and problems—to overcome beastly bad habits. So get up and help others. God will reward you for it!

devotion #52

BIG BRAGGING MOABITE MAN

Now Mesha king of Moab raised sheep . . . But after Ahab died, the king of Moab rebelled against the king of Israel.

— 2 Kings 3:4 – 5

At one time, Israel ruled over ancient Moab. After Israel's king died, Mesha, the king of Moab, rebelled and stopped paying his taxes, which included 100,000 lambs a year! Ever heard of the Moabite Stone? Well, in 1868 a German missionary found a stone tablet east of the Dead Sea. Guess who wrote it? It was none other than Mesha, king of Moab. It was his version of his big rebellion.

This stone tablet confirms what the Bible says — that Israel ruled over Moab and that Mesha led a rebellion.

The writing on the stone details Mesha's successes. He just, *um*, left out a few details, like the Israelites marching back to *re*-conquer him — led by the prophet Elisha, no less!

Ever had an older brother or cousin thump on you, but when you tell an adult about it, the kid's version sounds a lot different than yours? But a smart adult can sometimes see through the edited versions. If the kid says, "Yeah, I might have touched him, but he took my manga book!" See, now the kid just backed up your story, though he probably left out some facts. Same with Mesha.

People constantly find ancient objects and writings that back up what the Bible says. When you've even got Israel's *enemies* admitting that, well yeah, the Bible told the truth, you can't just sweep the story under the rug.

Devotion #53

HOLDING ONTO CLUES AND KEYS

"If you hold to my teaching, you are really my disciples. Then you will know the truth, and the truth will set you free."

— John 8:31 – 32

Many things in this world are true. It's true that gravity acts on all objects, and it's true that 3 + 4 = 7. But the most important truths are spiritual truths, such as the fact that Jesus died on the cross to save you. Jesus also taught a lot more truth about loving God and loving others. Hang onto his teachings. You'll know the truth, and it'll free you. How does that work?

It's like a video game where you're trying to find your way through some lost city. You have to remember certain clues to find hidden passageways, and you have to hang onto keys to open doorways. So your little character is running along — pitter-patter, pitter-patter — trying to find the way. And how do you find the passages? By remembering the clues you were given. How do you open the doors? By holding onto the keys you were given.

You have to seriously follow Jesus' teachings — not simply *hear* them, nod your head, and say, "Yeah, that's true." Do you want to avoid the traps and temptations of this world? Do you want to find your way? Do you want to be free? Then know the truth, remember it, and use it to solve problems. Receive Jesus' teachings, and hold onto them.

When you know the truth and obey it, it frees you from doubt and fear and worry and confusion. It sets you free.

devotion #54

EATING AWAY YOUR PEACE OF MIND

Do not be anxious about anything, but in everything, by prayer and petition, with thanksgiving, present your requests to God.

— Philippians 4:6

When the Bible says don't be anxious, it means don't worry and be fearful. Worried thoughts nibble at the edge of your mind and eat up your peace, so God tells you flat out, "*Don't* worry about anything!"

You know how your mom saves you a piece of cake for after school, but your little sister keeps going to the fridge and taking a little nibble here, a little nibble there . . . until, by the time you get home, your entire piece of cake has been devoured? Worry devours your peace of mind like your sister devours that piece of cake. What kind of things are you worried about? Your family's finances? A big test? Some kid who harasses you? Being late to a friend's house?

If you find yourself worrying or pacing or biting your nails, stop immediately! Drag that worry to God and pray about it — not just the big worries but the little ones too. God isn't going to groan even if you bring a piddly concern to him. After all, the Bible says, "Cast all your anxiety on him because he cares for you" (1 Peter 5:7). God cares about it all. (By the way, when the verse tells you to *petition* God, this is a one-person petition. You don't need a thousand signatures on your prayer before you present it to God. Just pray.)

Don't let worry eat your peace of mind. God doesn't want you to worry. He cares for you, so hand your anxious thoughts over to him.

devotion #55

WATER BUFFALOS, BUTTERFLIES, AND YOU

"In his hand is the life of every creature and the breath of all mankind."

—Job 12:10

Think how much power God has and how much he cares for us! All life on earth, from each big muddy water buffalo to every tiny butterfly—including all six and a half billion people on this planet—are in the palm of God's hand. God decides when every bit of life is born, and he decides the moment it will die. God is totally in charge of life.

People like to think they're independent and don't need God. Some say, "Sure I believe God exists, but I'm not going to worship him." Yet God created this whole world and everything in it. Look at the beautiful world he created. God created the complicated web of life and all the

systems that work so amazingly together. God created your mind that allows you to understand and appreciate what he has done. He's the one who gives you life and breath each day. Do you need God? Yes, you do. Of course you should worship him! How can you not be in awe of such a wonderful God!

The sooner we realize how much he cares for us and how much we need him, the better off we'll be. Not even one tiny sparrow dies unless it's God's will, so he's surely looking after you. Though God has created a big and complicated world, he loves us and knows about everything that happens to us.

Every day you live is a gift from God. Does he care for you? Yes. Is he close to you? He sure is! Your breath is in his hands.

Devotion #56

PUTTING THE BEST THINGS FIRST

I consider everything a loss compared to the surpassing greatness of knowing Christ Jesus my Lord.... I consider them rubbish.

— Philippians 3:8

As a kid, the apostle Paul received a top education in a Greek school. He studied poets and philosophers. As a young man, he studied under the top religious teachers in Israel. Paul tried to be the best he could be by obeying every tiny religious rule. But after Jesus saved him, he realized that, compared to knowing Jesus, all his accomplishments weren't worth much. He considered them rubbish.

When you are focused on a goal, such as a race or a homework assign-ment, you don't carry a big old black plastic bag of rubbish with you, do you? No. You drop the garbage off at the curb. And even if other good, cool stuff in your life isn't garbage, it can distract you from getting important stuff done. There is a time for computer games, TV, and hanging out with friends. They are all good and fun activities, but you can't do them while you're trying to play soccer or study for a test. Then they're dead weight, like garbage.

Paul enjoyed good food. He enjoyed talking with friends. He encouraged Christians to do their life's work well. But neither things nor money nor knowledge can be life's number-one goal. Good stuff is good stuff, yes. Life is good, yes. But if you put any of those things ahead of knowing Jesus, you just lost the main event — knowing Jesus and living for the truth.

Enjoy life. Enjoy the fun and games. But remember, the main purpose of a Christian is to know God and his Son, Jesus. Don't let anything get in the way of that.

devotion #57

SERVING GOD FOR REAL

"If God will be with me and will watch over me on this journey I am taking and will give me food to eat and clothes to wear . . . then the LORD will be my God."

— Genesis 28:20 – 21

Jacob had lived at home long after he had become an adult, eating his parents' food, wearing the clothes they provided, and coasting along on his dad's faith. Jacob knew about God, sure, but he'd never really depended on God — never given his heart to him. Now he was on his own and in trouble, so he began praying. He realized he needed a relationship with God.

A lot of kids raised in Christian homes are like that. They know all about God and they've heard the Bible stories, but until they face life's tests, they never really devote themselves to God. Then they get in a situation that's bigger than they are. They have to handle things without Mom or Dad coming to the rescue, and they start taking God seriously.

After a while, Jacob realized that God really was looking out for him. Then he began praying to God more and asking for help with his problems. And God came through every time! See, God loves it when we pray to him, whether we're in desperate situations or not. He wants you to realize that he really is God and that he has the power to take care of you.

God wants to look out for you, so start a relationship with him. Don't wait till you're in a tough situation to start praying. Pray today.

devotion #58

HAVING A MEAL WITH JESUS

"I stand at the door and knock. If anyone hears my voice and opens the door, I will come in and eat with him, and he with me."

— Revelation 3:20

In this verse, it sounds like Jesus is knocking on your bedroom door and wants to come in and eat pizza with you and get crumbs on your floor and drip tomato paste on your bed. Sounds good, but you know your mom doesn't go for eating in your room! In the Bible, when people talked about sharing a meal, it had a deeper meaning. It meant being good friends, spending time with people, and talking with them.

It's important to pick good friends. You don't just invite anyone

over to your house, right? And you certainly don't let just anyone in your room — just your best friends. And Jesus wants to be your best friend. Actually, more like a big brother. Not the kind who pounds on you, but the kind who always looks out for you.

By the way, Jesus isn't really standing knocking at your bedroom door. This verse is talking about the door to your heart — your whole life. And he's not just coming for a visit. He wants to come in and live with you from now on. The apostle Paul said, "I pray that . . . Christ may dwell in your hearts through faith" (Ephesians 3:16 – 17). But you need to invite him into your life.

Jesus wants to always be part of your life, be close to you, and help you and give you peace. So listen to his knocking and let him in.

devotion #59

LION ON THE LOOSE

Be self-controlled and alert. Your enemy the devil prowls around like a roaring lion looking for someone to devour. Resist him, standing firm in the faith.

—1 Peter 5:8–9

The Bible warns, "Be alert!" In other words, watch out, because the devil is as fierce and as dangerous as a man-eating lion on the loose. He's looking for his next lunch. Don't let him ambush you. So what do you do when he attacks? Run? No. Even though he roars to scare you, stand firm. "Resist the devil, and he will flee from you" (James 4:7).

One of the devil's favorite tricks is to ambush you with temptation. But you can control yourself. It helps to decide ahead of time that you won't give in to temptation. Then you won't be caught off guard. Now, Jesus will protect you if you stay close to him. He will help you be strong so you can stand with your decisions.

Stand firm in your faith, resist temptation, resist the devil, and he will flee from you. And remember, it's not like you're so strong that you can resist the devil on your own. No, when you resist the devil's temptations, it is because he is fleeing from Jesus, who is inside you. It's Jesus who makes the devil afraid. Having Jesus close to you is like having a powerful security guard watching out for you. The devil may still be growling as he flees, but he will flee.

Keep on guard for the devil's attacks. If he does attack, stand firm and resist him. You have the authority of Jesus to resist the devil. Do it, and he'll turn tail and run!

Devotion #60

WHY GOD GAVE PROPHECIES

These things happened so that the scripture would be fulfilled: "Not one of his bones will be broken," and, as another scripture says, "They will look on the one they have pierced."

— John 19:36–37

Hundreds of years before Jesus was born, God gave his prophets many prophecies about Jesus — and those things came to pass. For example, you know that Jesus was crucified, right? Now, when the Romans wanted a crucified man to die quickly, they broke his legs. But since Jesus was *already* dead, they didn't break his bones. Instead, they pierced his side with a spear. Two prophecies fulfilled at once!

So what does this mean to you? Well, it shows that God was thinking of *you* when he wrote the Bible. He knew you'd have questions like, "What proof is there that God exists? Is Jesus really who he said he was?" So right when the Bible was being written — centuries before Jesus was even born — God included some prophecies to help convince curious kids like you.

There's more: King David wrote Psalm 22 a thousand years before Jesus' birth — back before people even practiced crucifixion — yet that prophetic psalm perfectly describes what happened to Jesus when he was on the cross, with his arms being pulled out of joint. (See Matthew 27:32–50.) And if you really want your brain boggled, read Isaiah chapter 53. It was written six hundred years before Jesus, yet explains that he would die to forgive our sins.

Fulfilled Bible prophecies are proof that God exists and that Jesus is the Savior of the world. And there *are* lots of these fulfilled prophecies in the Bible!

devotion #61

WOW! REVELATIONS FROM THE BIBLE

Open my eyes that I may see wonderful things in your law.

— Psalm 119:18

We don't know who wrote this prayer. King David didn't sign his name to this psalm, so it probably wasn't him. But whoever it was, he considered God's Word his greatest treasure. To him, the Scriptures were like a gold mine. He was constantly digging in them. Sure, he'd read them many times, but he prayed for God to open his eyes so he could see wonderful stuff there that he'd never seen before.

Ever been looking for an eraser or a pencil sharpener and you just can't find it? Then your mom walks in the room and points it out to you, like, in five seconds? It was there all along, but you just

didn't see it. Well, God's Spirit is like a supermom who can show you stuff in the Bible. God can reveal stuff even to you. You just need to let him open your eyes.

Jesus promised, "The Holy Spirit . . . will teach you all things" (John 14:26). Of course, the Holy Spirit usually uses the Bible to teach you. Let's say you've read John chapter 15 a dozen times already, but then God lifts your eyelids, and suddenly it's like you're reading it for the first time. A verse you've read before jumps out at you and suddenly makes sense. Then you say, "Wow! I never saw that before!" You just saw wonderful things in God's Word.

Don't just read your Bible half-asleep because it's something you must do. Ask God to open your eyes and make the read worthwhile.

devotion #62

BECOMING MORE LIKE JESUS

When Moses came down from Mount Sinai . . . he was not aware that his face was radiant because he had spoken with the LORD.

— Exodus 34:29

Moses climbed up to the top of Mount Sinai and spent forty days and forty nights there, talking to God. After the Lord gave Moses the Ten Commandments, he sent Moses back down the mountain to the Israelites. Moses showed up and suddenly everyone was backing away, afraid to come near. He didn't realize that his face was glowing with God's glory.

If you spend time praying and reading your Bible, God begins to change you, and you become radiant too. You won't start glowing as bright as Moses did, but you will change. You may be saying, "Hold on! This is talking about holy people like missionaries and people who pray all day — not kids like me! God doesn't give skateboarders and computer gamers a touch of glory, does he? Does he?"

Oh yeah, he does. You may not think you radiate much of God's presence, but if you're a Christian, his Holy Spirit lives in you. And God's Spirit is constantly changing you, making you more like Jesus all the time. Instead of walking around full of anger or hate or fear, you'll have God's peace and joy in your face. Even if you can't see it, others will.

Spend time with God and read your Bible and meditate on it. God's Spirit inside you will become more evident in your life. You will change. Guaranteed.

devotion #63

GIVING GENEROUSLY TO GOD

Each man should give what he has decided in his heart to give, not reluctantly or under compulsion, for God loves a cheerful giver.

— 2 Corinthians 9:7

Giving is an important part of being a Christian. Jesus taught that his followers should give money to help the poor. The early disciples knew that they should give to help other Christians who were in need. Also, Christians should support pastors and missionaries. "The Lord has commanded that those who preach the gospel should receive their living from the gospel" (1 Corinthians 9:14).

In most churches, the offering basket is passed down the aisle every

Sunday. Maybe it has sailed past you week after week and you haven't paid much attention to it. (Ho-hum. Just a basket full of holy money.) But think about it: There are lots of needs in your church, and taking care of these needs costs money. Who pays for them? That's where you come in.

When you give to your church, you're helping the poor and helping your pastor and missionaries preach the gospel. Decide in your heart what you think you can afford to give and what you feel God wants you to give. Really think and pray about it. Don't give "under compulsion," meaning don't just give because you feel forced to. Instead, be generous and happy about giving.

Think about what you should give, decide on an amount, and then stick to your decision. Remember, God loves it when you give cheerfully! Your cheerfulness is part of the gift you give.

Devotion #64

KEEP AT IT! DON'T STOP PRAYING!

Elijah was a man just like us. He prayed earnestly that it would not rain, and it did not rain on the land for three and a half years. Again he prayed, and the heavens gave rain.

— James 5:17–18

Elijah bent down to the ground and put his face between his knees and prayed for rain wholeheartedly. (You don't have to be *that* flexible to pray, by the way.) Six times he sent his servant to go see if there were any rain clouds. Six times the guy returned and said, "Nothing." Elijah kept at it, and finally the servant came back with news of a cloud. Next thing you know there was a gully-washer!

Have you been praying for something but it hasn't happened yet — like you need to earn money to buy a bike? Or maybe you're sick, or someone close to you is sick? If the answer takes a while, you sometimes get discouraged and give up, right? You wonder why God doesn't answer. Maybe you ask yourself, "Doesn't God care?"

We're so impatient. We're used to doing a drive-through at MacBurger's, not even getting out of the car. We put in our order and pick it up a few minutes later. We get so many things in life immediately that it's hard to wait. But don't give up if your prayers aren't answered right away. God heard you, but he's not a fast-food chef.

Since the prophet "Elijah was a man just like us," and God answered his prayers, that means we can pray earnestly too, and *we* can get miraculous answers. Keep praying!

devotion #65

GHOSTS ON THE LOOSE?

When they saw him walking on the lake, they thought he was a ghost. They cried out, because they all saw him and were terrified.

— Mark 6:49 – 50

In Bible times, people thought that when someone died their spirit went down into the earth. Some superstitious people worried that unhappy spirits could come back to cause trouble. When Jesus' disciples were crossing the Sea of Galilee and they saw Jesus walking on the waves, they were sure he was a ghost. They were wrong. When Jesus showed up after he had been crucified, *again* they thought they were seeing a ghost. *Again* they were wrong (Luke 24:37 – 39).

Some people today believe that after a person dies his or her spirit wanders around and seeks revenge or maybe haunts houses. So if the wind slams a door or the cat steps on a squeaky floorboard, they let out a gasp, thinking it's a ghost. The Bible warns that if God's people disobey him, they'll end up so jittery that they'll be spooked by a rustling leaf and run when no one's even chasing (Leviticus 26:36).

The Bible does not teach that people's spirits wander around like spooks after they die. When Christians die, their spirits go to heaven. When the unsaved die, they go to hell. (Didn't know that? Hey, check out Luke 16:22–23.) The only kind of spirits that go around causing trouble are evil spirits — demons — and you can command them to leave in Jesus' name.

Believe in the Bible and trust in the power of the name of Jesus, and you won't need to fear creaking floorboards, slamming windows, and fluttering leaves.

Devotion #66

BADLY MISTAKEN THINKING

Jesus replied, "Are you not in error because you do not know the Scriptures or the power of God? . . . You are badly mistaken!"

— Mark 12:24, 27

Jesus taught that one day God would raise people's bodies back to life. The righteous will live with God forever; the evil will end up in the other place. Now, some religious leaders called Sadducees (*sad-you-sees*) didn't believe in the resurrection. They thought that once a person died, that was it — no heaven, no hell. Jesus said they were mistaken because they didn't know what the Bible taught.

A lot of people today have badly mistaken ideas because they don't

read the Bible. They just guess what it says, and they guess wrong — or else they get their ideas from TV shows and movies. Here are some common errors: Everyone goes to heaven. People turn into angels when they die. After a short stay in heaven, you reincarnate and come back to earth. Witches have "magical powers" from God.

It's great that someone invented television. Otherwise, what would we use TV clickers for? It's great that videos and CDs exist and that animators use computer programs to make cool kids' movies. And yes, there are great movies out there. But guys! Don't get your whole spiritual education from cartoons and movies. That's what the Bible's for.

If you don't want to end up with weird, mistaken ideas rattling around in your head like an out-of-control pinball machine, sit down and read the Bible.

devotion #67

GETTING A GLORIOUS BODY

Our citizenship is in heaven. And we eagerly await a Savior from there, the Lord Jesus Christ, who . . . will transform our lowly bodies so that they will be like his glorious body.

— Philippians 3:20 – 21

Eagerly wait, all right! Our Savior will come from heaven one day, and you are going to get a body that can power up and shine like the sun, step through solid walls, and never die. Jesus will change our ordinary bodies so that they're glorious like his body. (Want to know what Jesus' body is like now? Read Revelation 1:13 – 16.)

You've seen Transformer toys that start with an action figure, and you zippo-chango-rearrange the parts and

turn it into a car or a beast, right? Or maybe you get tired of the way your Lego models look, so you find a Website that tells you how to totally rearrange the pieces, and you redesign your bricks into a super-cool model.

Right now our bodies are like the original models, but they'll go through an astonishing change and become super bodies! "We will all be changed — in a flash, in the twinkling of an eye. . . . The dead will be raised imperishable" (1 Corinthians 15:51 – 52). Being raised imperishable means we'll never perish. We'll live forever with God. And not just live forever, dude, but forever with *power*!

It's already fantastic that Jesus is returning in all his glory, but when he has transformed *us*, we'll have awesome bodies with all new features and powers. We'll be able to do stuff we've never done before. That's also worth eagerly waiting for.

devotion #68

TAKING A SPIRITUAL SHOWER

Let us draw near to God . . . having our hearts sprinkled to cleanse us from a guilty conscience and having our bodies washed with pure water.

— Hebrews 10:22

Okay, this is not talking about taking a shower before you pray — though that's not a bad idea if you just came out of a mud-wrestling competition. This verse is saying that when Jesus forgives your sins he cleanses your mind. Then you no longer have a guilty conscience. You're washed and showered and you can approach God without worrying that you stink.

If you're like most kids, you probably think you're not "holy" enough to pray about serious things. Or maybe you think God won't give the time of day to someone who goofs up like you do. Sometimes when you go to pray, all you can think about is the last selfish thing that you did, so you figure God's not going to answer your prayers. Not true.

If you have asked Jesus to forgive your sins and save you, then you are clean. You don't need to have a guilty conscience and keep dragging a big bag of your sins and mistakes in your mind. If you have sincerely told God you're sorry, then he has forgiven you. And if you've sinned recently — like today — then sincerely ask God to forgive you for that too. He'll wash you clean. Then you can draw near to him . . . no sweat.

Have you asked God to sprinkle your heart today? If not, take a spiritual shower right now. Let God wash any dirt out of your life.

devotion #69

PUTTING ON THE ARMOR OF LIGHT

The night is nearly over; the day is almost here. So let us put aside the deeds of darkness and put on the armor of light.

— Romans 13:12

Obeying the Word of God is like waking up and getting dressed. When this verse says "the night is nearly over," it means that the world's present evil age has almost ended. "The day is almost here" means Jesus is coming soon. It's time to get dressed. But remember, in order to put on the armor of light, you first have to put aside the deeds of darkness. Wake up and stop doing things that displease God.

You've seen those cartoon shows where heroes of the future prepare for battle. All they do is think, *Armor on*, and suddenly these plates of shining armor begin whipping out of nowhere and snap in place all over their bodies. Within seconds, they're covered. Maybe you wish you could dress like that in the morning, instead of struggling to button your shirt when you're half-asleep — then finding that you buttoned it wrong.

God's armor is the most fantastic kind of battle armor. You pray for his Spirit to cover you with all the pieces of his armor, and he does. But you also need to grab the weapons he gives, like the Sword of the Spirit. You won't be able to see these things with your eyes though. God's armor is armor of light, all right, but *spiritual* light. (Read all about it in Ephesians 6:10 – 17.)

You want to be one of God's warriors? Then ditch the deeds of darkness, put on the armor of light, and get serious about being one of his fighters.

devotion #70

MAKING SOME PRIVATE SPACE

Jesus did not want anyone to know where they were, because he was teaching his disciples.

— Mark 9:30–31

Jesus loved people, but sometimes crowds practically mobbed him. Talk about no privacy! One time, Jesus and his disciples were in a house trying to have a meal, but such a large crowd pushed in around them that they weren't able to eat (Mark 3:20). Imagine being so squeezed you can't get your fork to your mouth! You can't live like that. So when Jesus wanted to teach his followers, they had to slip off to some quiet place.

Now, you probably don't have to escape into the Mojave Desert to read

your Bible or pray. Hopefully a sign on your bedroom door will give you the space you need. But the point is you *do* need quiet space. And you can be "mobbed" by outside noise even in your bedroom if music is playing or if some virtual pet is beeping to be fed.

The word *disciple* means "someone who follows the Master's teaching." Hopefully, you're trying to do that. And the news is Jesus still teaches his followers today. How does he do that? As you read God's Word, he teaches you and shows you amazing stuff. And when you pray, the Holy Spirit reminds you of what you've read and leads you in the right direction.

Take a break! Get away from all the cartoons and noise and distractions. Let Jesus teach you. Jesus said, "Learn from me . . . and you will find rest for your souls" (Matthew 11:29).

devotion #71

MUSTARD AND MULBERRY MIRACLES

"If you have faith as small as a mustard seed, you can say to this mulberry tree, 'Be uprooted and planted in the sea,' and it will obey you."

— Luke 17:6

One day, Jesus' disciples asked him to increase their faith. They knew they didn't have great faith. But Jesus told them that even if they had a *little* faith, it could accomplish great things. The mustard seed was a very tiny seed, yet when it grew up, it became huge. Just like a tiny seed grows into something mighty, just a bit of faith can do great things.

Maybe you feel like your faith isn't strong, so you don't bother to pray.

But Jesus' advice applies to you too. Do you need an obnoxious kid to leave you alone? Do you need a better memory for homework — or even to *find* your homework? Pray. God can do great things. Just don't pray for things God never meant for you to have — like your own flying saucer. It isn't always easy to know if you are being greedy or out of line in what you ask for. Pray for things that your heart tells you are best, and ask if it's his *will* for you to have those things. Now, very few people have the faith to command a mulberry tree to rip its roots out of the ground and drop itself into the sea. But do you get what Jesus was saying? God can do astonishing miracles. (After all, he created the world and the entire universe out of nothing.) You just have to pray and believe that he'll answer you.

If mulberry miracles are possible, then surely God can do less dramatic miracles for you. Even if you think your faith isn't super great, pray.

devotion #72

GOD ISN'T JUST LIKE YOU

"I am God, your God. . . . You thought I was altogether like you."

— Psalm 50:7, 21

Back in Old Testament times, many Israelites preferred to worship idols of false gods and goddesses that looked like tiny clay humans. And they gave these "gods" personalities. They quarreled, were selfish, and liked all the sinful stuff that selfish humans liked. In other words, the people liked gods who were just like *them*. Go figure!

So is the eternal, unchanging God just like you? No way. The Lord of heaven and earth is who he is. He is God. The trouble is that lots of people don't like how the Bible describes God. For example, they don't think he should judge them for their sins. So what do they do? They say he doesn't *mind* their sin. They "remake" God. By the time they're done, they've invented a God who's a lot like them and who approves of the things they like.

Only problem is that's not God. That's a cheap imitation. God does not look like the reflection in your mirror. He is not "altogether like you." If he were just like you, he wouldn't be God. Want a good idea of what the Lord is like? Read your Bible. God is exactly who he is and — like it or not — no amount of wishful thinking will change him.

God is the unchanging, eternally existing Lord of heaven and earth. You can't control him. You can't give him a makeover. All you can do is worship and obey him.

Devotion #73

BUMPED OFF THE PATH

You were running a good race. Who cut in on you and kept you from obeying the truth?

— Galatians 5:7

Two thousand years ago, Paul traveled to the Roman province of Galatia and preached to the Galatians that faith in Jesus — faith and nothing else — saved them. The Galatians believed this, but later some teachers persuaded them that faith wasn't enough; they *also* had to keep all the complicated laws of Moses. Paul was upset. The Galatians had been running a good race. Now they were stumbling off track.

Ever been running and have someone cut in front of you, forcing

you to slow down and lose your stride? Next thing you know you're falling behind. Or ever been riding downtown with your mom and some driver cuts in front of her without signaling? She hits the brakes, lays about twenty feet of rubber, and you make a nose-dent in the seat in front of you. Someone just cut in on you.

Living the Christian life is like running a race. But often when you're flying along, making good time, the devil sends one of his messengers to cut in on you. He wants to bump you so you'll run off the path. He sends along a temptation to distract you or some weird teaching to trip you up and slow you down. Watch out. Don't get ambushed.

Keep running the good race. Obey God's truth, and don't let anyone cut in on you. Don't even listen to weird stuff that'll get you off track from the truth.

devotion #74

GROWING OUT OF ELEMENTARY GRADES

You need someone to teach you the elementary truths of God's word all over again. . . . Let us leave the elementary teachings about Christ and go on to maturity, not laying again the foundation.

— Hebrews 5:12; 6:1

Back in the days of the early church, some teachers wanted Christians to learn new things and move on to the next grade. Problem was, many people still hadn't gotten the elementary lessons. They were still struggling to get the basic, foundational truths down — like why they should love others, why they needed to repent for their sins, or why Christians should be baptized.

It's like if you invite a friend over to play a video game and, to your surprise, the guy has *no clue* which buttons are for "jump" or "attack." He can't even make the character run right or left. His character is stuck against some wall. His little feet are flying, but he's not getting anywhere. Your friend doesn't have the foundations of the game. You need to teach him and help him move on to the next level so he can actually play the game.

If you're a Christian, it's important to learn the basics about your faith so you'll know what you believe about Jesus and why you believe it. Then you'll know how to live. So how do you learn the basics? Well, listen during Sunday school. Grab a Bible storybook. Best of all, read your Bible and think about what it's saying. If you come to a part you don't understand, ask someone who knows.

God wants you to learn the basics so that you can move from the elementary teachings to other stuff you need to know. Do you have the basics down?

devotion #75

THE HEAVENLY CITY

The city does not need the sun or the moon to shine on it, for the glory of God gives it light, and the Lamb is its lamp.

— Revelation 21:23

The Bible describes heaven as a magnificent city with streets of gold, walls made of twelve different kinds of gems, a river of life with Trees of Life growing by it, and fabulous places to live! Now, how much of this is literal and how much is symbolic we don't know, but one thing we do know: our eternal home will be more wonderful than anything we can possibly imagine.

Maybe you've been to Disneyland and thought that was great!

Or maybe you've never been to Disneyland, but you've heard it's the place to go, and you'd like to check it out before going to heaven. Hey, if you miss Mickey, don't sweat it! Heaven will be so much better!

And where will you live? Jesus said, "In my Father's house are many rooms. . . . I am going there to prepare a place for you" (John 14:2). You'll be living with God! That's the best part: God himself will be there. There'll be no more pain or death or sorrow or crying — just happiness forever.

Heaven isn't a fairy tale or just some fluffy-puffy cloudland. Heaven is a very real, exciting place, and we'll be living there one day.

devotion #76

TEMPORARY TROUBLE, HUGE REWARDS

Our light and momentary troubles are achieving for us an eternal glory that far outweighs them all.

— 2 Corinthians 4:17

Back in Paul's day, Christians were often persecuted for their faith. People hated them, told lies about them, spat on them, and gave them grief. Sometimes Christians lost their jobs just because of their faith, and they didn't know where they'd get money. Paul knew these troubles were real. After all, he'd suffered a lot himself. But he reminded Christians that these troubles were light because their heavenly rewards would far outweigh the trouble.

It's no fun going through difficult times. Maybe you've lost a good

friend or you've been injured. Or maybe your parents are having a hard time financially and you can't afford things that other kids enjoy. Or maybe kids who were once your friends tease you because you believe in Jesus. It may not seem like your troubles are light. They may seem sandbag-heavy.

But God promises that when you suffer here on earth in his name, he will repay you with heavenly rewards, with "an eternal glory that far outweighs them all." Those eternal rewards won't just outweigh your troubles, they'll *far* outweigh them. It would be like if you missed out on a lollipop now but got a dirt bike in three months. It's worth the wait.

Sometimes when you're going through troubles, it's not easy to keep your eyes on the ultimate goal — heaven. It's not easy to tell yourself that it will be worth it all. But just the same, it will be worth it all.

devotion #77

WITNESSING AND ALLIGATORS

"Go into all the world and preach the good news to all creation."

— Mark 16:15

Jesus' disciples were enthusiastic about the fact that Jesus had died to save them from sin. Why? Because Jesus hadn't *stayed* dead! He was resurrected. He conquered death itself, and by doing this, he proved that he could give eternal life to everyone who believed in him. Then Jesus told his disciples to go into all the world and preach this good news to everyone. Thousands of Christians got excited about this news because it *is* terrifically good news.

Think about it like this: if you discovered a brand new TV show and it had the coolest characters with awesome graphics and action, but none of your friends knew about it, you'd be excited to tell them what channel it was on and what time it ran, right? Or if some kid was giving away free baby alligators, you'd tell all your friends about it, right? Well, your friends don't really need an alligator, but they do need Jesus.

The word *gospel* means "good news," and in Jesus' day, Christians obeyed Jesus and preached the good news. Christians are still doing it today. Maybe your church has missionaries in far-away nations. But, do you know what? Even Hometown, U.S.A., is part of "all the world," and people in your city need to hear about Jesus too, right? So tell them!

You don't have to be a Bible expert or a missionary to tell others about Jesus! You don't have to go to a far-away country. Tell your friends what you *know* or invite them to church.

devotion #78

WHY THE GOSPELS WERE WRITTEN

These are written that you may believe that Jesus is the Christ, the Son of God, and that by believing you might have life in his name.

— John 20:31

After Jesus died, he showed himself to his disciples and gave them many proofs that he had come back to life. For example, Thomas said he wouldn't believe it was really Jesus unless he put his finger in the holes where the nails had been. Jesus showed up and said, "Put your finger here; see my hands." That convinced Thomas, and because this story was written down, it can encourage our faith as well. (See John 20:24–28.)

You may wonder why it's so important to read your Bible regularly, or to spend time each day reading devotional books. You might think, "I've *heard* these stories in Sunday school. I *know* them. Why read them again?" Or you may wonder, "I already believe in Jesus, so I *already* have eternal life. So do I really need to read the Bible?"

You not only need eternal life, but reading and believing God's Word gives you the spiritual strength to face the troubles of *this* life also. Jesus said, "I have come that they may have life, and have it to the full" (John 10:10). Why struggle along in your own strength? Live life to the fullest! Besides, the purpose of reading devotions is to *devote* yourself to God, and that starts by getting his Word deep in your heart.

The Bible is full of amazing stories and miracles. Read it today, and let God's Holy Spirit fill your heart with faith.

devotion #79

A DROP IN THE BUCKET

The nations are like a drop in a bucket; they are regarded as dust . . . they are regarded by him as worthless and less than nothing.

— Isaiah 40:15, 17

God is so big that we can't even imagine how huge he is. He's bigger than the universe itself. Solomon said that "the heavens, even the highest heavens, cannot contain him" (2 Chronicles 2:6). God is bigger than a gazillion galaxies put together. No yardstick can even begin to measure God. And he's not just immense size-wise. He's also all-powerful, and his understanding is infinite.

No wonder that, compared to God, even powerful nations like the

United States seem like a drop in the bucket. Even large countries like Australia are regarded as dust. And you gotta wonder, if great nations are like worthless specks of dust, what about you? Um . . . I guess that'd make you smaller than a microbe on a dust speck. Okaaay, next question: If you're so microscopic, why would God care for you?

As nothing as people are — as tiny and less-than-dust sized as we happen to be — God cares for us. He loves us so much that he created this whole world just for us to live on. (It's big to us, at least!) He loves people so much that he sent his only Son, Jesus, to come down to this dusty, peewee-sized planet and live among us microbes . . . er, people.

The nations may be a drop in the bucket. They may be worthless dust. But eensy-teeny people are worth a great deal! You are very valuable to God.

devotion #80

IT'S NOT LUCK

"Joseph is no more and Simeon is no more, and now you want to take Benjamin. Everything is against me!"

— Genesis 42:36

You can understand poor old Jacob thinking that everything was against him. As far as he knew, his son Joseph was dead, his son Simeon was in prison, and now he risked losing his youngest son, Benjamin. But the truth was, Joseph was alive, Simeon was fine, and Ben was in no danger. This wasn't a case of "bad luck" or everything being against him. We know from the rest of the story that God was in control and working things out to Jacob's benefit — although it certainly didn't seem that way to him.

Ever had a string of bad stuff happen and you say, "I'm having bad luck"? Some kids try to get good luck and keep away bad luck by carrying around lucky charms or lucky pennies. Is God okay with that?

No, we know he's not. He said he was against magic charms (Ezekiel 13:20). God wants people to know that *he* is in control of their destiny, not lucky charms. And even if God allows tough things to happen, it's for a good purpose. Or if bad stuff is happening because you're disobeying God, then repent, start obeying, and pray — and God can turn things around!

When it seems like everything is against you, remember: it has nothing to do with luck. God is the one who's in control of your life.

devotion #81

YOU KNOW WHAT I'M TALKING ABOUT

"The king is familiar with these things, and I can speak freely to him. I am convinced that none of this has escaped his notice, because it was not done in a corner."

— Acts 26:26

When Paul was talking to King Agrippa about Jesus, Paul said he was glad that he could speak freely to the king. He didn't have to stop and explain who Jesus was, what he had done, or that he had died on the cross. Paul didn't have to remind Agrippa that when Jesus died, "darkness came over the whole land" for three hours (Mark 15:33).

The king knew all these things. Everyone in Israel did. Jesus had been headline news.

Since they couldn't deny the basic facts, some imaginative people tried to explain them away. For example, a Roman historian named Thallus wrote a history book about twenty years after Jesus died. He admitted that okay, yes, there *had* been this incredible darkness, but it was probably just an eclipse of the sun. (Nice try, Thallus! But Jesus was crucified at Passover when there was a full moon. Eclipses never happen on a full moon.)

Lots of people today might be clueless about Jesus, but back in those days, everybody in Israel knew who he was. No one denied that Jesus had actually lived. ("Hello! What planet are *you* from?") No one questioned that Pontius Pilate had crucified Jesus. No one denied that Jesus' tomb was empty. These were well-known facts.

This is the cool thing: Christianity is based on facts. Jesus lived and died and came back to life in real time in real history.

devotion #82

TAKE TIME TO CHEW

"I have treasured the words of his mouth more than my daily bread."

— Job 23:12

Job was an old, super-wealthy wise man who lived a long time ago in the desert kingdom of Uz. In fact, he lived *so* long ago that only the first bit of the Bible existed — the book of *Genesis*. Yet Job treasured that one book more than all his jewels and gold and camels and land. He treasured it more than his daily bread, because bread kept him alive *physically*, but God's Word gave *spiritual* life.

You gotta eat good food to stay strong and healthy. But while you're chewing your cereal, remember that God's words are even more important. So take time to read your Bible.

While you're munching your lunch, remember to snack on a Scripture "power bar." Just a few verses can pack a lot of energy. When you sit down to dig into dinner, be thankful for the Bible.

Jesus said to pray, "Give us today our daily bread," but he also said, "Man does not live on bread alone, but on every word that comes from the mouth of God" (Matthew 4:4; 6:11). You need food to live, but you can't stuff your face with sandwiches and think that's all you need. You need to feed yourself spiritually. If you've never read the Bible on your own, start reading it today.

Job's Bible had only one book in it, yet Job considered it his greatest treasure — more important than food. You have the whole Bible — an entire banquet. Dig in!

devotion #83

WHEN GOD ANSWERS NO

"I had it in my heart to build a house . . . and I made plans to build it. But God said to me, 'You are not to build a house for my Name.' "

— 1 Chronicles 28:2–3

King David wanted to build a temple for God and when he asked God's prophet Nathan about it, Nathan thought a second then answered, "Whatever you have in mind, go ahead and do it, for the LORD is with you" (2 Samuel 7:3). Oh yeah! *That's* the kind of answer we like. But that night when Nathan prayed about it, God told him no, David was *not* to build a temple.

Sometimes your requests to God seem perfectly reasonable — like asking

God to make your plans work out, or asking him to supply the money for summer camp. You think, "Well, I'm doing my best to obey God, so of course he's going to give me a yes answer." But you pray, and God either doesn't do it, or else he does something different than you expected. What do you make of that?

Sometimes it's just not the right time for whatever you're praying for. Or maybe, even if what you want is a good thing, God knows that it wouldn't be the best for you. In King David's case, God had other plans for David and made him some terrific promises, so David was okay with not building the temple. Solomon built it instead.

Remember, God is God. He's in charge. He doesn't have to answer yes to everything you desire, but he will do what's best for you.

devotion #84

FUN TRIVIA VERSUS WORTHLESS IDOLS

"They followed worthless idols and became worthless themselves."

—Jeremiah 2:5

Back in Jeremiah's day, many people turned their backs on God—the one who gave them life and blessed them with good things—and began praying to dead idols. Since they were living their lives to please worthless idols, the people's lives ended up being worthless.

This might make you worry. "Wait a second. Lots of stuff I'm interested in—like collecting stamps or cartoon books or baseball cards—don't really have spiritual value, but I think they're cool!" Does God want you to give up your hobbies? If it doesn't have

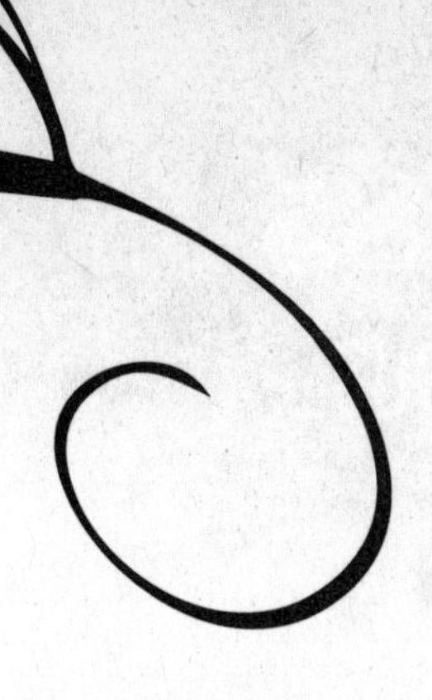

spiritual value and doesn't draw you closer to God, is it a worthless idol?

No, it's not. You can enjoy your personal interests. Stamps are cool. Cartoons are funny. Baseball cards are interesting. God gave you a brain and a personality so you can use them. God doesn't want you to make any of those things the center of your life, but you're probably not in danger of doing that. Some people make money the center of their lives. They would do anything to get more money—even things they know are wrong. Money is useful and important, but if you make money more important than God or your relationships with others, it'll leave you empty. Also, be careful about how you act about pop idols or movie stars. If following their interests and careers makes you turn your back on God or make bad decisions, then they're worthless role models.

You can enjoy trivia and collect cartoon books and stuff. And music and videos are fun. Just don't follow worthless stuff that takes you away from God. Love God and you'll have a truly worthwhile life.

devotion #85

DON'T BE SUPERSTITIOUS

They are full of superstitions from the East; they practice divination like the Philistines.

— Isaiah 2:6

The Israelites were often tempted to copycat the superstitious customs of the nations around them — the Philistines to the west and the Arameans to the east. When they needed direction and it seemed that God took too long to answer their prayers, they turned to mediums and sorcerers to divine (figure out) what to do. They also began believing in silly stuff like wearing lucky amulets and medallions to keep evil spirits away.

Many people today are just as superstitious. They carry rabbit feet

around with them, figuring that a dead bunny paw will bring them good luck. They flip their lucky penny every time they need a yes or no answer. They're afraid of the number thirteen and freak if a black cat crosses their path. (You gotta wonder why there are no superstitions about black Labs.)

As Christians, we serve the all-powerful God, and our future is in his hands. Our fate isn't in the hands of some non-existent Lady Luck. We don't need rabbit feet to bring good luck and keep bad luck away. God has promised that if we love and trust him, that he will lead us the way we should go, and he will protect us from evil and bless us.

God's answers sometimes take a while to come, but that's because he wants to teach us to trust him and follow the Bible, faithfully. So ditch silly superstitions, and listen to God.

devotion #86

GETTING GROUNDED BY GOD

Jonah was inside the fish three days and three nights. From inside the fish Jonah prayed to the LORD his God.

—Jonah 1:17; 2:1

You know the story: Jonah disobeyed God and ran, so God had a monster fish swallow him. Jonah spent days sloshing back and forth in saliva, gagging and groaning—and probably barfing too. Do you know what happens to a chunk of meat in a fish's stomach? It gets digested. Next thing Jonah knew, gallons of digestive juice and stomach acids were pouring down at him. Acid? You know *that's* gotta sting!

Have you ever disobeyed God and ended up swallowed by a giant fish? Not likely. But maybe you were disrespectful to your parents and were sent to your room. Or you fooled around with the wrong crowd, doing the wrong things, and you were grounded for a week. It's not just your parents who have the power to punish you, by the way. The older you get, the more God deals with you personally.

It's important to obey your parents, but you should determine to please God as well. God doesn't like to punish you or take away privileges in your life, and as long as you obey him, he doesn't need to. But if he needs to, God definitely will "ground" you in some way to get your attention. He wants to help you see that you need to obey.

When Jonah repented, God forgave him and gave him another chance. The monster fish puked him onto dry land. So the next time you're having some time out, try praying for God's forgiveness. God heard Jonah from a fish's gut. He can hear you too.

devotion #87

LISTENING TO GOD'S BREATHING

All Scripture is God-breathed and is useful for teaching, rebuking, correcting and training in righteousness.

— 2 Timothy 3:16

Scripture means the "writings of the Old Testament." It also means the gospels about Jesus and the letters of the apostles in the New Testament. God inspired it all. God's breath, his Holy Spirit, fills every page. That's why you should let the Bible teach you what's right, rebuke you when you sin, correct you when you make mistakes, and train you how to live a godly life.

Lots of books today have good advice. The book that tells you how to program your new TV comes with good advice — what you can understand of it. Once in a while, even cartoon books have some good lessons in them. Come to think of it, even kids' TV shows have at least one good moral per show — usually something like, "Be nice to others." You can learn how to be a better person from many different books — fiction and nonfiction.

So is the Bible like other books? Was it just written by people to teach other people some practical information about life? No. People can give messed-up advice. The Bible gives solid, guiding truths. Men wrote it, but God's Holy Spirit inspired them to write it — from the first verse in Genesis that says God created the world to the last verses in Revelation that promise Jesus is coming back.

You want to know what God thinks about something? Read the Bible. Want to obey God and do what's right? Obey the Scriptures. God's Spirit inspired — breathed into — them.

devotion #88

JUNKING JUNK, POUNDING IDOLS

He tore down the altars and the Asherah poles and crushed the idols to powder and cut to pieces all the incense altars throughout Israel.

— 2 Chronicles 34:7

Josiah was a young king who wanted to do what was right in God's eyes. Many Jews had stopped worshiping God and were bowing down to idols of the demon gods, Baal and Asherah. So Josiah started a spiritual revolution. He tore down the altars of Baal. He smashed the wooden carvings of Asherah. He hammered the stone idols to pieces and then pounded the pieces to powder.

There probably aren't any stone idols of Baal in your town, but lots of

things can be like idols. This does not mean you should grab a sledgehammer and go after your neighbor's lawn ornaments. You are not responsible for other people's yards, so leave the gnomes alone. What you are responsible for is cleaning up any idols in your own life.

Look around your bedroom. Check under your mattress. Check out your walls. See any bad stuff you need to get rid of? Now, just because you like something a lot doesn't mean that it has become an idol. You can have posters of music stars or sports stars on your wall. The problem comes when they stand for values that are against God and your faith. Then you gotta send them packing.

Josiah broke the idols to pieces and then crushed them to dust to show that he was serious about getting rid of idols. No one worships dust, right? If you have junk to junk, junk it today.

devotion #89

RULING NATIONS - OUR DESTINY

To him who overcomes and does my will to the end, I will give authority over the nations.

— Revelation 2:26

Jesus knew that Christians would be constantly tempted to compromise and disobey and live selfishly, so he made a terrific promise: If his followers were faithful to overcome their sins and do what was right, he would greatly reward them. The most faithful would be given authority over entire nations. To have *authority* means Christians will "reign on the earth" (Revelation 5:10). And of course, there'll be rulers under them who govern states and cities and towns.

Have you ever watched news on TV and been discouraged about what a mess the world is in? Have you ever wished that judges and governors and rulers would start treating people fairly and do what was right? Have you ever wished honest people could rule the world for a while? Well, one day that's going to happen. After Jesus returns, he will set up his kingdom on earth and pick godly people to run every part of this planet.

God's kingdom won't be like those games where you're the king of the castle and you get to boss all the other kids around and make them tie your shoes and be your slaves. Christians will rule, yes, but Jesus said that if you want to be a ruler, you have to first learn how to serve people and care about them (Mark 10:42–44). You govern others well by doing what's best for them.

Learn to look out for other people, overcome your problems, and one day when Jesus' Kingdom has come on earth, you will be ready for power and responsibility.

Devotion #90

FEASTING WITH THE FAMOUS

Many will come from the east and the west, and will take their places at the feast with Abraham, Isaac and Jacob in the kingdom of heaven.

— Matthew 8:11

In Jesus' day, the Jews believed that God would one day raise all the Israelites back to life, and the righteous would enjoy eternal life in God's kingdom. Part of their reward was that they'd sit down at huge tables and enjoy a fantastic feast. But Jesus said that there wouldn't just be Jews at the feast — but also *non*-Israelites from all over the world.

Ever been invited to a dinner with a famous celebrity, like maybe a

sports hero or someone else you really admire? The food is great, the company's great, and you're having a great time! Or hey, even if it's not a banquet, maybe it's a great feast like Thanksgiving or Christmas, or a family reunion or picnic, and you get to enjoy mouth-watering food and spend time with long-lost cousins.

One of the very cool things about heaven is that we'll be reunited forever with saved loved ones. On top of that, tons of amazing Christians who have lived for the past two thousand years will be there. And we'll also be sitting down to eat with Abraham and Isaac and Jacob and other men and women straight out of the pages of the Bible.

One day, every believer who has ever lived will be invited to a great feast (Revelation 19:9). Make sure *you* believe in Jesus so there's a place reserved for you!

Luke 2:52

Perfect for boys, the 2:52 series is based on Luke 2:52: "And Jesus grew in wisdom and stature, and in favor with God and men." Focusing on four primary areas of growth, this guiding verse can help boys become more like Jesus mentally (smarter), physically (stronger), spiritually (deeper), and socially (cooler). From Bibles and devotionals to fiction and nonfiction, with plenty of gross and gory mixed in, there is something for every boy.

Visit www.Luke252.com

deborahjdg4

We want to hear from you. Please send your comments about this book to us in care of zreview@zondervan.com. Thank you.

ZONDERVAN.com/
AUTHORTRACKER
follow your favorite authors